# Billy Liar

A comedy

# Keith Waterhouse
and
Willis Hall

Samuel French — London
New York - Toronto - Hollywood

D1343242

Please see page iv for further copyright information

# BILLY LIAR

This play was first presented at the Cambridge Theatre, London, on 13th September 1960, with the following cast:

| | |
|---|---|
| **Florence Boothroyd** | Ethel Griffies |
| **Geoffrey Fisher** | George A. Cooper |
| **Alice Fisher** | Mona Washbourne |
| **Billy Fisher** | Albert Finney |
| **Arthur Crabtree** | Trevor Bannister |
| **Barbara** | Ann Beach |
| **Rita** | Juliet Cooke |
| **Liz** | Jennifer Jayne |

Directed by Lindsay Anderson

The play is set in Stradhoughton, an industrial town in the north of England in 1960

ACT I
Saturday morning

ACT I
Afternoon of the same day

ACT III
Later the same evening

No character, in this play, is intended to portray any specific person, alive or dead.

The running time of this play, excluding intervals, is two hours and ten minutes.

## PRODUCTION NOTE

Taken at its face value, *Billy Liar* could be produced as a simple comedy about a boy who tells lies. There is, however, much more in it than this and the rewarding production will be the one that realizes the strong dramatic theme which lies below the surface. Beneath the comedy runs the story of an imaginative youth fighting to get out of his complacent, cliché-ridden background. The director should not regard Billy as being a freak or a buffoon; the life of fantasy which he lives exists in most people but perhaps Billy's fantasies are nearer to the surface than most. The snatches of fantasy-life which are seen in the play should be directed for reality rather than comedy, and with subtlety rather than with the heavy hand which would take it dangerously near to farce. A production in which Billy is directed purely for laughs in the first two acts will find its audience unprepared to accept the serious content of the third act when Billy, for a time, sheds his final skins of make-believe.

Although Billy is the central character, his importance in the play can be seen only in contrast to his stolid family, and so it is important that his father, his mother and his grandmother should be seen as real persons and not as feeds. Similarly with the three girls it is necessary that Barbara and Rita should not be caricatures but should, in fact, be as real as Liz. On first reading of the text it will be seen that many of the lines are very funny — it must be appreciated however that the same lines are carefully naturalistic. It is this naturalism that the director should aim for in production. It may help the director to read the original novel on which the play was based.

Billy must remember that although he is very different from the rest of his family he is still a member of it. He has the family accent and the family mannerisms. Even when falling into fantasy his accent should not change all that much. For example, in the officer fantasy in Act III, Billy will find that he will get a better effect by being a northern boy trying to imitate officer-class accents than by being the accomplished actor giving a skilful imitation of an officer. Billy will find that the overall balance of the play hangs largely upon himself and it will be up to him to carry over the difficult transition of the play from Act II to Act III. It is important therefore that Billy's early fantasy scenes are not played as a kind of vaudeville act in an attempt to get as many laughs as possible. Billy must always remember that the purpose of all his fantasy scenes is to give the audience a key to what is going on in his mind.

Geoffrey is a more complex person than the blustering character who appears in Act I. The actor playing Geoffrey might find it helpful to study first the scene in Act II in which Geoffrey tries to make some contact with Billy; he could then build up the character from this point rather than superimpose this facet of Geoffrey's character on a standard blustering performance. The word "bloody" — which Geoffrey uses repeatedly — may give some trouble if it is used as an expletive and not as an unconscious punctuation mark in Geoffrey's dialogue. In the case of some amateur societies where the use of the word at all is likely to give offence, the authors give permission for it to be deleted completely — but not for the substitution of euphemisms such as "ruddy" "blooming", etc.

Alice is probably the least difficult of the characters to assess. She is a simple uncomplicated woman who has set her values many years ago and never re-examines them, not even in the most extraordinary circumstances. In her evaluation of other people's character she can see no further than the externals — personal appearance, manner of speech, etc. But it will be found that the role of Alice is very important for she is, so to speak, the hub of the circle of people we see in this play. All the arguments revolve around her; nothing takes place in the play that will not affect her in one way or another. Alice, for all her soft-centred, self-indulgent outlook is in fact a strong woman and should be cast as such.

Florence is a role which could easily tempt an actress to play a comic cameo without reference to the play at large. Little of Florence's dialogue is sparked off by other characters; she spends most of her time rambling to herself. This is not to say, however, that Florence does not react to what is going on around her. We must feel all the time that she belongs in the family and we should get the impression that she hears a great deal more than she appears to do. We must not get the impression that her daydreams bear any similarity to Billy's fantasies, for when Florence goes into musings they are confined only to the hard realities of her past.

Barbara, although on one level a stolid, bovine character, is in her own way a fantasist just as much as Billy, for she lives in a woman's magazine world of thatched cottages and tweedy pipe-smoking heroes. Her reaction to Rita arises not too much out of jealousy at a rival as out of revulsion at having to face a side of life not normally on view through her rose-coloured spectacles.

Rita is a difficult character to play in that she has been written deliberately on one note, and a high note at that. The fact is that Rita is a simple, extrovert girl who does not change radically in any given situation. The way in which the actress playing this part should use her skill is in reproducing as accurately as possible the raucous irreverence of this type of working-class girl.

Liz, as can easily be seen, is the character closest to Billy in outlook and temperament. In spite of what we hear about her habits of flitting off from time to time she is not in any way a fey character, but has a down-to-earth quality which she tries to transmit to Billy. Although economically a member of the same class as Billy and his family, she has an outlook transcending its narrow boundaries and lower middle-class traits are not as apparent in her. The most important thing about Liz is that she should radiate warmth and generosity; but in playing her scene with Billy she should remember — as indeed Billy should remember — that this is a scene not about two people in love but two people who are trying to get love from each other.

Arthur is more than a feed for Billy. All ample study of the part will reveal that there is a strong character change in Arthur as the play progresses. He begins in sympathy with Billy and his ideas but, lacking Billy's majestic sweep of vision, he grows jealous and impatient as the play moves along.

The characters in *Billy Liar* — with the exception of working-class Rita — come from a lower middle-class background in an industrial town. They should not have the broad "Ee bah goom" accents of a mill town, mining town, or other closed northern community, but the simple broad accents of the provinces.

The lighting of the play is very important, especially in the third act. The lighting follows two conventions: the living-room is lit with complete naturalism — standard lamps, overhead light, etc.; but Billy's garden scene in Act III, where the only natural light is that from the street lamp, gives the producer the opportunity to use his lighting to underline Billy's escape into a world of fantasy. The best effect, when Billy is discovered alone in the garden, is probably to start the scene in the naturalistic evening light of the garden and then, as Billy begins his "officers and gentlemen" soliloquy, to diminish the lighting gradually until, when we come to the Last Post, Billy is standing in the light of a single spot.

The large set of living-room, hall and garden may pose something of a problem on smaller stages. In such cases it is suggested that the garden scenes be played on the bare stage in front of the living-room, and the garden seat dispensed with. The lighting, of course, should be appropriately changed.

Keith Waterhouse   Willis Hall

# ACT I

*The set consists of a living-room, entrance hall and a section of the garden of Geoffrey Fisher's house. It is a typical lower middle-class detached house in an industrial town in the north of England. To the left of the stage is the garden containing a small garden seat. The entrance to the house from the garden leads directly into the hallway with stairs going up to the bedrooms. Through the hallway is the living-room where most of the action of the play takes place. There is also a door in the living-room R, leading into the kitchen. The room is furnished with an uncut moquette three-piece suite and a dining-room suite in dark oak. The furniture is quite new, but in dreadful taste — as are also the plaster ornaments and the wall plaques with which the room is over-dressed. Above the fireplace is the usual collection of family photographs on the mantelpiece and above the mantelpiece is a large brass-studded circular mirror. The room also contains a cheap and flashy cocktail cabinet, a large television set and also a sideboard with two cupboards*

*As the* CURTAIN *rises we discover Florence Boothroyd sitting on the couch. She is Alice Fisher's mother, an old lady in her eighties, who finds it impossible to accustom herself to the modern way of life. She continually talks to herself and when she cannot be heard her lips continue to move. She is in the habit of addressing her remarks to inanimate objects. At the moment she is going through the contents of her large handbag. The handbag is open on her knee and as she takes out each object she examines it and then puts it down on the couch beside her, making a neat display. She has already taken out a few odd possessions and, at the moment, she is holding her old-age pension book. She addresses the sideboard*

**Florence** I don't know ... They haven't stamped my book now ... They haven't sent it up. It should have gone up last week but they haven't sent it up. (*She puts down the pension book and takes a white hospital appointment card from her handbag*) That's not right, either. Doctor Blakemore? I've never seen Doctor Blakemore. Which is Doctor Blakemore? I bet it's that black doctor. Else it's the lady doctor. I'm not seeing her. Tuesday? They know I never go on Tuesdays. I've never been on Tuesday yet. Doctor Thorpe said ...

*It comes to her that she is alone in the room. Putting down the handbag she rises and crosses slowly and flat-footed to the sideboard. She attempts to open the right-hand cupboard but, discovering it is locked, returns to the couch and again takes up her handbag*

He's as bad. And she encourages him. He lives in that bed. *(Noting the appointment card on the couch she picks it up)* And where's that crepe bandage they were going to get me. *(She puts down the card)* What's he always keep it locked up for, anyroad? There's neither sense nor reason in that. And she never tells you anything.

*Alice Fisher, Geoffrey's wife, enters from the kitchen. She is a woman in her middle forties. Both Alice and her husband have had working class upbringings, but Geoffrey's success as a garage owner has moved them up into this new stratum of society. At the moment Alice is caught up in the normal day-to-day rush of breakfast-time. She is speaking to her husband who is in the kitchen*

**Alice** Well, you do what you think fit, Geoffrey. Do what you like — it's no good me saying anything. But I know what I'd do. He still owes you for that last job you did for him.

*Alice crosses the room towards the hall, ignoring her mother who speaks to her as she passes*

**Florence** Who's Doctor Blakemore? Which one is that, then? Is that the one you went to?
**Alice** *(entering the hall, calling up the stairs)* It's time we were having you down, my lad. That bedroom clock's not fast, you know. It's half-past nine turned.

*Alice turns and enters the living-room*

**Florence** I'll bet it's that black doctor, isn't it? I'll bet it's him.
**Alice** Who? Blakemore? Yes, I think it is.
**Florence** I'm not seeing him. I shan't go. I shall stop at home.
**Alice** If they say you've got to see him—you've got to see him, Mother. It's no good arguing. That's all there is to it.

*Geoffrey Fisher enters from the kitchen. He is a tall man in his early fifties. He is carrying a few invoices and, crossing and seating himself in an armchair, he begins to go through them*

**Florence** They caused all that bother on the buses in Birmingham. And Egypt. Mau-Mau. I make no wonder Eden's always so badly. And him upstairs. He's just as bad. I think it's time his father talked to him. I don't know why he puts up with it. I can't understand why he lets him carry on like that.

**Geoffrey** (*looking up from the invoices he speaks to Alice. In his speech he uses the adjective "bloody" so frequently that it becomes completely meaningless*) It's all right you talking, Alice, you don't understand. I've got no bloody choice. I can't turn work away.

**Alice** I've said what I've got to say. I'm not saying anything. I'm keeping out of it.

**Florence** They let him carry on just as he likes. I wouldn't. I'd see to him.

**Geoffrey** Where's his bloody lordship, then?

**Florence** I'd tell her. She lets him lead her on. She wants to go up to him with a wet dish-cloth and wring it over his face. That'll get him up.

**Geoffrey** He wants a bloody good hiding.

**Florence** ... that'd move him ...

**Alice** I've shouted him three times.

**Florence** ... that'd shift him ...

**Geoffrey** It's every morning alike.

**Florence** ... he'd have to get up then.

**Geoffrey** You let him do just as he likes!

*Alice takes up the poker and a small shovel from the fireplace and crosses into the hall*

**Alice** (*calling up the stairs*) Billy! ... Billy! (*She bangs the poker against the shovel*) I shan't tell you again. If I come up there you'll know about it! I suppose you know what time it is! Your boiled egg's stone cold and I'm not cooking another.

**Florence** She lets him do just as he likes.

**Geoffrey** Go up to him. Go up and kick him out. He's bloody idle!

*Alice returns into the living-room and places the poker and shovel back into the fireplace*

**Alice** It's all right you sitting there. You don't stand need to talk. You haven't emptied them ashes yet.

**Florence** She wants to go up to him. I would. (*She is now returning the objects to her handbag and pauses when she comes to the appointment card*) It's a mystery to me about that crepe bandage. I know I had it. It's in this house somewhere.

**Geoffrey** You can't put anything down in this house. Not without somebody bloody shifting it. And who keeps taking my invoices out of that vase? Somebody bloody does.

**Florence** He ought to see that window's properly locked every night. He never bolts that back door properly. It wants doing. There's all sorts moving around when it gets dark.

*Billy Fisher begins to come down the bedroom stairs. He is nineteen years old and slightly built. He is wearing an old raincoat over his pyjamas. He is smoking a cigarette*

**Alice** Is that him? He's stirred himself at last, then. I'll see what his breakfast is doing.

*Alice goes out to the kitchen as Billy reaches the foot of the stairs. Billy takes the morning paper from behind the door and enters the living-room*

**Florence** She lets him do just as he likes.

**Billy** (*reading aloud from the paper*) Cabinet Changes Imminent.

**Geoffrey** Yes, and you'll be bloody imminent if you don't start getting up on a morning.

**Billy** Good morning, Father.

**Geoffrey** Never mind bloody good mornings. It's bloody afternoon more like. If you think your mother's got nothing better to do than go round cooking six breakfasts every morning you've got another think coming.

**Florence** She lets him do what he wants.

**Billy** (*ignoring his father he turns and bows, acting out the situation to his grandmother*) Your servant, ma'am.

**Geoffrey** And you stop that bloody game. I'm talking to you. You're bloody hopeless. And you can start getting bloody well dressed before you come down in the morning.

**Florence** He wants to burn that raincoat. He wants to burn it. Sling it on the fire-back. Then he'll have to get dressed whether or no.

**Billy** I gather that he who would burn the raincoat is Father and he who should get dressed of a morning is my good self. Why do you always address all your remarks to the sideboard, Grandmother?

**Geoffrey** (*almost rising from his chair*) Here, here, here! Who do you think you're bloody talking to? You're not out with your daft mates now. And what time did you get in last night? If it was night. This bloody morning, more like.

*Alice enters from the kitchen*

**Billy** I really couldn't say. 'bout half-past eleven, quarter to twelve. Good morning, Mother.

**Geoffrey** More like one o'clock, with your bloody half-past eleven! Well, you can bloody well start coming in of a night-time. I'm not having you gallivanting round at all hours, not at your bloody age.

**Billy** Who are you having gallivanting around, then?

**Geoffrey** And I'm not having any of your bloody lip. I'll tell you that, for a start.

**Alice** What were you doing down at Foley Bottoms at nine o'clock last night?

**Billy** Who says I was down at Foley Bottoms?

**Alice** Never mind who says, or who doesn't say. That's got nothing to do with it. You were there — somebody saw you. And it wasn't that Barbara you were with, either.

**Florence** He wants to make up his mind who he is going with.

**Geoffrey** He knocks about with too many lasses. He's out with a different one every night. He's like a bloody lass himself.

**Billy** Well, you want to tell whoever saw me to mind their own fizzing business.

**Alice** It is our business — and don't you be so cheeky. You're not old enough for that.

**Florence** If she's coming for her tea this afternoon she wants to tell her. If she doesn't I will.

**Billy** I suppose that she who's coming for her tea is Barbara and she who wants to tell her is Mother and ——

**Alice** I've told you — shut up. I'm going to tell her, don't you fret yourself. You've never played fair with that girl. Carrying on. I'm surprised she bothers with you. You shouldn't mess her about like that. One and then the other. That's no way to carry on. I know where you'll finish up — you'll finish up with none of them — that's where you'll finish up.

**Geoffrey** He'll finish up on his bloody ear-hole. I'm not having him staying out half the night. Not at his age. He's not old enough. He'll wait till he's twenty-one before he starts them bloody tricks. I've told him before, he can start coming in of a night or else go and live somewhere else.

**Billy** Perhaps I will do.

**Alice** (*ignoring him*) I can't understand that Barbara — why she does bother with you. Are you supposed to be getting engaged to her or aren't you?

**Geoffrey** He doesn't know who he's bloody getting engaged to.

**Florence** He wants to make his mind up.

**Alice** (*ignoring Geoffrey and Florence*) Because she's not like these others, you know. That time I saw you in the arcade with her she looked respectable to me. Not like that Liz or whatever her name is. That scruffy one you reckoned to be going about with. Her in that mucky skirt. Do you ever see anything of her still?

**Geoffrey** He sees so many bloody lasses he doesn't know who he does see.

**Florence** He wants to make his mind up — once and for all. He wants to make his mind up who he is going with.

**Billy** I haven't seen Liz for three months.

**Alice** Well, who were you with then? Down at Foley Bottoms? Last night?

**Billy** Rita.

**Geoffrey** Who the bloody hell's Rita?

**Florence** She wants to see that he makes his mind up.

**Alice** I shall tell Barbara this afternoon — I shall tell her, make no mistake about that.

**Geoffrey** He's never satisfied with what he has got — that's his bloody trouble. He never has been. It's ever since he left school. It's ever since he took that job — clerking. Clerking for that undertaker — what kind of a bloody job's that

**Billy** Perhaps I might not be doing it much longer.

**Geoffrey** You what?

**Alice** What do you mean?

**Billy** I've been offered a job in London.

**Geoffrey** (*turning away in disgust*) Don't talk bloody wet.

**Alice** How do you mean? A job in London? What job in London?

**Billy** (*taking a crumpled envelope from his raincoat pocket*) What I say, I've been offered a job in London. Script-writing.

**Geoffrey** Bloody script-writing.

**Alice** What script-writing?

**Geoffrey** Script-writing! He can't write his bloody name so you can read it. Who'd set him on?

**Billy** (*proudly*) Danny Boon.

**Alice** Danny who?

**Billy** (*going into a slow, exasperated explanation*) I told you before. Boon. Danny Boon. I told you. He was on at the Empire the week before last. When he was there I told you. I went to see him. I went to his dressing-room. I took him some of my scripts. Well, he's read them. He's read them and he likes them. And he's sent me this letter. He's offered me a job in London. Script-writing. Danny Boon. The comedian. He's been on television.

**Florence** (*addressing the television*) It's always boxing; boxing and horse shows.

**Alice** (*ignoring her*) Danny Boon? I don't remember ever seeing him.

**Geoffrey** No, and neither does anybody else. It's another of his tales. Danny Boon! He's made him up.

**Alice** What kind of a job?

**Billy** I've told you. Script-writing.

**Geoffrey** It's like all these other tales he comes home with. He can't say two words to anybody without it's a bloody lie. And what's he been telling that woman in the fish shop about me having my leg off? Do I look as though I've had my leg off?

**Billy** It wasn't you. It was Barbara's uncle. She gets everything wrong — that woman in the fish shop.

**Alice** You'll have to stop all this making things up, Billy. There's no sense in it at your age. We never know where we are with you. I mean, you're too old for things like that now.

**Billy** (*displaying the letter*) Look — all right then. I've got the letter — here. He wants me to go down to see him. In London. To fix things up. I'm going to ring up this morning and give them my notice.

**Alice** You can't do things like that, Billy. You can't just go dashing off to London on spec.

**Geoffrey** (*disparagingly*) He's not going to no bloody London. It's them that'll be ringing him up, more like. You'll get the sack — I'll tell you what you'll get. What time are you supposed to be going in there this morning, anyroad?

**Billy** I'm not. It's my Saturday off this week.

**Geoffrey** You said that last bloody week. That's three bloody weeks in a row.

**Billy** I got mixed up.

**Geoffrey** I've no patience with you. (*He places the invoices in his pocket and rises from his chair*) Anyway, I've got some work to do if you haven't.

**Alice** Are you going in towards town, Geoffrey?

**Geoffrey** I'm going in that direction.

**Alice** You can drop me off. I'm going down as far as the shops.

**Geoffrey** I can if you're not going to be all bloody day getting ready. I'm late now.

**Alice** (*crossing towards the hall*) I'm ready now. I've only to slip my coat on.

*Alice goes out into the hall and puts on a coat which is hanging on the rack. Geoffrey turns to Billy*

**Geoffrey** And you can get your mucky self washed — and get bloody dressed. And keep your bloody hands off my razor else you'll know about it.

**Florence** (*raising her voice*) Is she going past Driver's? 'Cause there's that pork pie to pick up for this afternoon's tea.

**Alice** (*entering the living-room*) I'm ready. I'll call in for that pie. (*To Billy*) Your breakfast's on the kitchen table. It'll be clap cold by now.

**Geoffrey** (*crossing towards the door; turning for a final sally at Billy*) And you can wash them pots up when you've finished. Don't leave it all for your mother.

**Alice** I shan't be above an hour, Mother.

*Alice and Geoffrey go out through the hall and into the garden. Billy goes into the kitchen*

**Florence** I shouldn't be left on my own. She's not said anything now about the insurance man. I don't know what to give him if he comes.

*Alice and Geoffrey are moving down the garden*

**Geoffrey** I'm only going as far as the lane, you know. I don't know why you can't get the bloody bus.

*Alice and Geoffrey exit*

*Billy enters from the kitchen He is carrying a cup and a teapot*

**Billy** I can't eat that egg. It's stone cold.
**Florence** There's too much waste in this house. It's all goodness just thrown down the sink. We had it to eat. When I was his age we couldn't leave nothing. If we didn't eat it then it was put out the next meal. When we had eggs, that was. We were lucky to get them. You had to make do with what there was. Bread and dripping.
**Billy** (*sitting down, pouring himself a cup of tea*) Do you want a cup of tea?
**Florence** And if you weren't down at six o'clock of a morning you didn't get that.

*Billy drinks and grimaces*

**Billy** They don't drink tea in London at this time of a morning. It's all coffee. That's what I'll be doing this time next week.
**Florence** Sundays was just the same. No lying-in then.

*Billy and his grandmother are now in their own separate dream-worlds*

**Billy** Sitting in a coffee-bar. Espresso. With a girl. Art student. Duffel-coat and dirty toe-nails. I discovered her the night before. Contemplating suicide.
**Florence** If you had a job in them days you had to stick to it. You couldn't get another.
**Billy** (*addressing his imaginary companion*) Nothing is as bad as it seems, my dear. Less than a week ago my father felt the same as you. Suicidal. He came round after the operation and looked down where his legs should have been. Nothing.
**Florence** We couldn't go traipsing off to London or anywhere else. If we got as far as Scarborough we were lucky.
**Billy** Just an empty space in the bed. Well, he'll never be World Champion now. A broken man on two tin legs.

*Billy slowly levers himself out of his chair and limps slowly and painfully around the room leaning heavily against the furniture*

**Florence** *(addressing Billy in the third person)* He's not right in the head.

*Billy realizes he is being watched and comes out of his fantasy*

I wouldn't care, but it makes me poorly watching him.
**Billy** *(rubbing his leg and by way of explanation)* Cramp.
**Florence** He wants to get his-self dressed.

*Arthur Crabtree enters the garden and approaches the front door. He is about the same age as Billy. He is wearing flannels, a sports coat and a loud checked shirt. He pushes the door-bell which rings out in two tones in the hall*

*As Billy crosses to answer the bell*

He shouldn't be going to the door dressed like that.

*Billy opens the door and, together with Arthur, goes into a routine — their usual way of greeting each other. Arthur holds up an imaginary lantern and peers into an imaginary darkness*

**Arthur** *(in a thick north-country accent)* There's trouble up at the mill.
**Billy** *(also in a thick north-country accent)* What's afoot, Ned Leather? Is Willy Arkwright smashing up my looms again?
**Arthur** It's the men! They'll not stand for that lad of yours down from Oxford and Cambridge.
**Billy** They'll stand for him and lump it. There's allus been an Oldroyd at Oldroyd's mill and there allus will be.
**Arthur** Nay, Josiah! He's upsetting them with his fancy college ways and they'll have none of it. They're on the march! They're coming up the drive!
**Billy** Into the house, Ned, and bar the door! We've got to remember our Sal's condition.

*They enter together and march into the living-room where they both dissolve into laughter*

**Florence** Carrying on and making a commotion. It's worse than Bedlam. Carrying on and all that noise. They want to make less noise, the pair of them.
**Arthur** Good morning, Mrs Boothroyd.

**Florence** He wants to make less noise and get his-self dressed.

**Billy** Do you want a cup of tea, Arthur? I'm just having my breakfast.

**Arthur** You rotten idle crow! Some of us have done a day's work already, you lazy get.

**Billy** Why aren't you at work now?

**Arthur** Why aren't you at rotten work, that's why I'm not at work. Come to see where you are. They're going bonkers at the office. You never turned in last Saturday either.

**Billy** Isn't it my Saturday off this week?

**Arthur** You know rotten well it isn't.

**Florence** (*getting up from the couch*) They're all idle. They're all the same. They make me badly.

*Florence crosses the room and disappears up the stairs into the bedroom*

**Billy** I could say I forgot and thought it was.

**Arthur** You can hellers like. You said that last week.

**Billy** Tell them my grandad's had his leg off.

**Arthur** You haven't got a rotten grandad. Anyroad, I can't tell them anything. I'm not supposed to have seen you. I've come up in my break. I'm supposed to be having my coffee. I'm not telling them anything. I'm having enough bother as it is with our old lady. What with you and your lousy stories. Telling everybody she was in the family way. She's heard about it. She says she's going to come up here and see your father.

**Billy** Cripes, she can't do that! It was only last night I told him she'd just had a miscarriage. She's not supposed to be up yet.

**Arthur** What the hell did you tell him that for?

**Billy** I hadn't any choice. My mother was going to send a present round for the baby.

**Arthur** The trouble with you, cocker, is you're just a rotten pathological liar. Anyway, you've done it this time. You've dropped yourself right in with not coming in this morning.

**Billy** I can get out of that. I'll think of some excuse.

**Arthur** There's more to it than that, matey. Shadrack's been going through your postage book.

**Billy** When?

**Arthur** This morning, when do you think? There's nearly three rotten quid short. All there is in the book is one stinking lousy rotten threepenny stamp and he says he gave you two pound ten stamp money on Wednesday.

**Billy** Fizzing hell! Has he been through the petty cash as well?

**Arthur** Not when I left. No. Why, have you been fiddling that as well?

**Billy** No, no . . . I haven't filled the book up, though.

**Arthur**  And he was going on about some calendars — I don't know what he meant.

**Billy**  (*crossing to the sideboard*) I do. (*He takes a small key from his raincoat pocket and opens the right-hand cupboard. As he does so a pile of large envelopes fall out on to the carpet followed by a few odds and ends*) There you are, Tosh, two hundred and sixty of the bastards.

**Arthur**  What?

**Billy**  Maring calendars.

**Arthur**  (*crossing and picking up an envelope from the floor*) What do you want with two rotten hundred and sixty calendars? (*Reading the address on the front of the envelope*) "The Mother Superior, The Convent of the Sacred Heart!" (*He tears open the envelope and takes out a large wall calendar illustrated with a colourful painting of a kitten and a dog. Reading the inscription*) "Shadrack and Duxbury, Funeral Furnishers." These are the firm's! "Taste, Tact and Economy." You skiving nit! You should have posted these last Christmas.

**Billy**  Yes.

**Arthur**  Well, what are they doing in your sideboard cupboard?

**Billy**  I never had enough stamps in the postage book.

**Arthur**  You think that postage money's part of your bloody wages, don't you? (*He bends down and sorts through the pile of papers on the floor*) Why do you keep them in there?

**Billy**  It's where I keep all my private things.

**Arthur**  (*picking up a small package*) Private things! A naffing crepe bandage! (*He throws down the package and picks up a piece of blue notepaper*) What's this then?

**Billy**  (*making a grab for the letter*) Gerroff, man! Give us that here! That's personal!

**Arthur**  (*evading Billy's hand*) What the hell are you writing to Godfrey Winn for?

**Billy**  It's not me. It's my mother.

**Arthur**  (*reading the letter*) "Dear Sir, Just a few lines to let you know how much I enjoy *Housewives' Choice* every day, I always listen no matter what I am doing, could you play 'Just a Song at Twilight' for me." That's a turn-up for the top ten! She isn't half with it, your old lady! (*Reading*) "I don't suppose you get time to play everyone that writes to you, but this is my favourite song. You see my husband often used to sing it when we were a bit younger than we are now. I will quite understand if you cannot play. Your respectfully Mrs A. Fisher." So why didn't you post this then?

**Billy**  I couldn't be bothered. (*He makes a further attempt to grab the letter*) Give us it here!

**Arthur**  (*holding him off*) "P.S. My son also writes songs, but I suppose there is not much chance for him as he has not had the training. We are just ordinary folk."

**Billy** *(snatching the letter and tossing it into the cupboard)* I'm not ordinary folk even if she is. *(He crams the envelopes containing the calendars back into the cupboard)* I keep trying to get rid of them. It was bad enough getting them out of the office.

**Arthur** How long have they been here?

**Billy** Not long. I used to keep them in that coffin in the basement at work. You can't get rid of the fizzing things! It's like a bloody nightmare. They won't burn. I've tried tearing them up and pushing them down the lavatory — all they do is float.

**Arthur** Makes no difference what you do with them. Duxbury's on to you. He knows about them.

**Billy** *(stuffing the last of the calendars into the cupboard and locking the door)* Oh well ... so what. He knows what he can do with his calendars. I don't give a monkey's. I'm leaving. I've got another job.

**Arthur** Leaving?

**Billy** I'm going to ring him up this morning and give him my notice.

**Arthur** Yes, and we've heard that one before.

**Billy** No, straight up. I'm going to London.

**Arthur** What as — road-sweeper?

**Billy** *(grandiloquently)* Ay road sweepah on the road — to fame! *(He returns to his normal voice)* I've got that job with Danny Boon.

**Arthur** You haven't!

**Billy** Yes — script-writer. Start next week.

**Arthur** You jammy burk! Have you though, honest?

**Billy** Yeh — course I have. It's all fixed up. He sent me a letter. Asking me to work for him.

**Arthur** What's he paying you?

**Billy** A cowing sight more than I get from Shadrack and flaming Duxbury's.

**Arthur** What? Counting the postage?

**Billy** What's it to you? This is it for me, boy! Success! "Saturday Night Spectacular!" "Sunday Night at the Palladium!" Script by!

**Arthur** Ta-ra-ra-raaa!

**Billy** Billy Fisher! Directed by!

**Arthur** Ta-ra-ra-raaa!

**Billy** William Fisher! Produced by!

**Arthur** Ta-ra-ra-raaa!

**Billy** William S. Fisher!

**Arthur** Ta-ra-ra-raaa!

**Billy** A W. S. Fisher Presentation! "Mr Fisher, on behalf of the British Television Industry, serving the needs of twenty million viewers, it gives me great pleasure to present you with this award, this evening, in recognition of the fact that you have been voted Television Script-writer of the Year — for the seventh year running."

**Arthur** (*picking up a vase from the sideboard he places it in Billy's hands*)
Big-head.
**Billy** (*returning the vase to the sideboard*) Rot off. You wait and see.
**Arthur** (*taking a small bottle of tablets from his trouser pocket*) So you
won't be needing these now, then, will you?
**Billy** What's them?
**Arthur** Passion pills. What I said I'd get for you.
**Billy** (*taking the bottle incredulously*) Let's have a look, mate. (*He opens the
bottle and is about to swallow one of the tablets*) What do they taste like?
**Arthur** Here, go steady on, man! They'll give you the screaming ab-dabs.
**Billy** (*returning the tablet to the bottle*) How did you get hold of them?
**Arthur**. From a mate of mine who got demobbed. He brought them back
from Singapore.
**Billy** I'll bet they're bloody aspirins.
**Arthur** Do you want to bet? You want to ask this bloke, tosher.
**Billy** How many do you give them?
**Arthur** Just one. Two two-and-nines at the Regal, a bag of chips and one of
these and you're away. Who's it for anyway?
**Billy** Barbara ... Bloody hell!
**Arthur** What's up?
**Billy** She's supposed to be coming round this morning.
**Arthur** I thought it was this afternoon? For her tea?
**Billy** (*placing the bottle of tablets on the sideboard*) No, I've got to see her
first. Our old man'll go bald if he sees her before I've had a word with her.
She thinks he's in the Merchant Navy.
**Arthur** You what?
**Billy** (*crossing hurriedly towards the hall*) On petrol tankers. (*He indicates
the tea-things*) Shift them into the kitchen for me. Shan't be a tick.

*Billy runs up the stairs in the hall and into his bedroom*

*Arthur picks up the teapot and goes into the kitchen. He re-enters and crosses
to the sideboard where he picks up the bottle of tablets*

*Billy appears at the top of the stairs with his clothes in his hands*

*Billy moves down the stairs and enters the living-room. Arthur replaces the
tablets on the sideboard.*

**Arthur** What time's she supposed to be coming?
**Billy** (*dressing hastily*) Quarter of an hour since. Where's them passion pills?
**Arthur** On the sideboard. You're not going to slip her one this morning are
you?

**Billy**  Why not? I'm pressed for time, man. I'm going out with Rita tonight.

**Arthur**  Well, what about your grandmother?

**Billy**  Oh, she's spark out till dinner-time.

**Arthur**  I've lost track of your rotten sex life. Which one are you supposed to be engaged to, anyway?

**Billy**  That's what they call an academic question.

**Arthur**  Well, you can't be engaged to both of them at once, for God's sake.

**Billy**  Do you want to bet?

**Arthur**  Crikey! Well, which one of them's got the naffing engagement ring?

**Billy**  Well, that's the trouble. That's partly the reason why Barbara's coming round this morning — if she did but know it. She's got it. I've got to get it off her. For Rita.

**Arthur**  What for?

**Billy**  Ah, well ... You see, she had it first — Rita. Only I got it from her to give to Barbara. Now she wants it back. I told her it was at the jeweller's — getting the stone fixed. There'll be hell to pay if she doesn't get it.

**Arthur**  The sooner you get to London the better.

**Billy**  (*tucking his shirt in his trousers and slipping on his jacket*) Are you sure them passion pills'll work on Barbara? She's dead from the neck down.

**Arthur**  You haven't tried.

**Billy**  Tried! Who hasn't tried! If you want to try you're welcome. All she does is sit and eat stinking oranges.

**Arthur**  What I can't work out is why you got engaged to her in the first place. What's wrong with Liz?

**Billy**  Don't talk to me about Liz. I've not seen her for months. She's tooled off to Bradford or somewhere.

**Arthur**  Well, she's tooled back again then. I saw her this morning.

**Billy**  What? Liz?

**Arthur**  Yeh — scruffy Lizzie. I bumped into her in Sheepgate. Mucky as ever. It's about time somebody bought her a new skirt.

*Barbara approaches the house. She is about nineteen years old, a large well-built girl in a tweed suit and flat-heeled shoes. She is carrying a large handbag*

**Billy**  Did she say anything about me?

**Arthur**  I didn't stop. Just said "Hallo". I wouldn't be seen stood standing talking to that scruffy-looking bird.

*Barbara rings the bell*

**Billy**  That's Barbara! Where's them passion pills!

*Billy crosses and, taking the bottle from the sideboard, he places it in his breast pocket. Arthur crosses toward the door*

**Arthur** I'll have to get going, anyway. I'll get shot when I get back to work. I've been gone nearly half an hour now.
**Billy** (*crossing towards the door*) Hang on a couple of minutes, man. Don't make it look too obvious! If she sees you going out and leaving her with me she'll be out of that door like a whippet.
**Arthur** I'm late now!
**Billy** You can chat her up for a minute.

*He crosses into the hall and opens the door to admit Barbara*

Hallo, darling!
**Barbara** (*who uses endearments coldly and flatly*) Hallo, pet.
**Billy** (*leading the way*) Come through into the lounge.
**Barbara** (*following Billy into the living-room*) Hallo, Arthur.

*Arthur winks at her. Barbara looks round the room*

What a nice room! (*She crosses to examine the cocktail cabinet*) What a beautiful cocktail cabinet!
**Billy** I made it.

*Arthur reacts to this statement*

**Barbara** How clever of you, sweet. I didn't know you could do woodwork.
**Billy** Oh yes, I made all the furniture. (*A pause and then, wildly*) And the garage.

*Barbara looks around the room doubtfully*

**Arthur** (*coughing*) It's time I was making a move, mate.
**Barbara** You're not going because of me, Arthur?
**Arthur** No, I'm supposed to be at work. (*To Billy*) So long, tosh!
**Billy** So long.
**Barbara** Bye! ... Isn't your sister in, Billy?
**Arthur** (*stopping short on his way to the door and turning*) What bloody sister?

*Billy, unnoticed by Barbara, gesticulates to Arthur to leave*

*Arthur does so — hastily*

**Billy** Barbara, I'm glad you asked me that question. About my sister.
**Barbara** What is it?
**Billy** Sit down, darling.

*Barbara sits on the couch*

Darling, are you still coming to tea this afternoon?
**Barbara** Of course.
**Billy** Because there are some things I want to tell you.
**Barbara** What things, Billy?
**Billy** You know what you said the other night — about loving me? Even if I were a criminal.
**Barbara** Well?
**Billy** You said you'd still love me even if I'd murdered your mother.
**Barbara** (*suspiciously*) Well?
**Billy** I wonder if you'll still love me when you hear what I've got to say. You see — well, you know that I've got a fairly vivid imagination, don't you?
**Barbara** Well, you have to have if you're going to be a script-writer, don't you?
**Billy** Well, being a script-writer, I'm perhaps — at times — a bit inclined to let my imagination run away with me. As you know.

*Barbara is even more aloof than usual*

You see, the thing is, if we're going to have our life together — and that cottage—and little Billy and little Barbara and the lily pond and all that ... Well, there's some things we've got to get cleared up.
**Barbara** What things?
**Billy** Some of the things I'm afraid I've been telling you.
**Barbara** Do you mean you've been telling me lies?
**Billy** Well, not lies exactly ... But I suppose I've been, well, exaggerating some things. Being a script-writer ... For instance, there's that business about my father. Him being a sea captain. On a petrol tanker.
**Barbara** You mean he's not on a petrol tanker?
**Billy** He's not even in the navy.
**Barbara** Well, what is he?
**Billy** He's in the removal business.
**Barbara** And what about him being a prisoner-of-war? And that tunnel? And the medal? Don't say that was all lies?
**Billy** Yes.

*Barbara turns away abruptly*

Are you cross?
**Barbara**. No — not cross. Just disappointed. It sounds as though you were ashamed of your father.

**Billy** I'm not ashamed. I'm not — I'm not!
**Barbara** Otherwise why say he was a prisoner-of-war? What was he?
**Billy** A conscientious ob ... (*He checks himself*) He wasn't anything. He wasn't fit. He has trouble with his knee.
**Barbara** The knee he's supposed to have been shot in, I suppose.
**Billy.** Yes. Another thing, we haven't got a budgie, or a cat. And I didn't make the furniture ... Not all of it, anyway.
**Barbara** How many other lies have you been telling me?
**Billy** My sister.
**Barbara** Don't tell me you haven't got a sister.
**Billy** I did have. But she's dead. If you're still coming for your tea this afternoon they never talk about her.

*Barbara remains silent, her head still turned away*

You remind me of her ... If you're not coming, I'll understand ... I'm just not good enough for you, Barbara ... If you want to give me the engagement ring back — I'll understand.
**Barbara** (*turning towards him*) Don't be cross with yourself, Billy. I forgive you.
**Billy** (*moving to kiss her*) Darling ...
**Barbara** (*moving away*) But promise me one thing.
**Billy** That I'll never lie to you again?

*Barbara nods*

I'll never lie to you again. Never, I promise ... Darling, there is one thing. I have got a grannie.
**Barbara** I believe you.
**Billy** Only she's not blind. She's not very well, though. She's upstairs. Sleeping. She might have to have her leg off.
**Barbara** (*kissing him*) Poor darling.
**Billy** (*moving quickly towards the cocktail cabinet*) Would you like a drink?
**Barbara** Not now, pet.
**Billy** (*opening the cabinet*) Port. To celebrate.
**Barbara** All right. Well, just a tiny one.
**Billy** I'm turning over a new leaf.

*Unnoticed to Barbara he pours the drinks and taking a tablet from the "passion pill" bottle, places it in her glass. He crosses with the glasses and sits beside her on the couch*

That's yours, darling.
**Barbara** (*sitting on the edge of the couch she sips the port*) Let's talk about something nice.

**Billy** Let's talk about our cottage.

**Barbara** Oh, I've seen the most marvellous material to make curtains for the living-room. Honestly, you'll love it. It's a sort of turquoise with lovely little squiggles like wine-glasses.

**Billy** Will it go with the yellow carpet?

**Barbara** No, but it will go with the grey rugs.

**Billy** (*taking her in his arms*) I love you, darling.

**Barbara** (*moving away*) I love you.

**Billy** Do you? Really and truly?

**Barbara** Of course I do.

**Billy** Are you looking forward to getting married?

*Barbara takes an orange from her handbag and peels it and eats it during the following dialogue*

**Barbara** I think about it every minute of the day.

**Billy** Darling ... (*He again attempts unsuccessfully to kiss her*) Don't ever fall in love with anybody else.

**Barbara** Let's talk about our cottage.

**Billy** (*simulating a dreamy voice*) What about our cottage?

**Barbara** About the garden. Tell me about the garden.

**Billy** We'll have a lovely garden. We'll have roses in it and daffodils and a lovely lawn with a swing for little Billy and little Barbara to play on. And we'll have our meals down by the lily pond in summer.

**Barbara** Do you think a lily pond is safe? What if the kiddies wandered too near and fell in?

**Billy** We'll build a wall round it. No — no, we won't. We won't have a pond at all. We'll have an old well. An old brick well where we draw the water. We'll make it our wishing well. Do you know what I'll wish?

**Barbara** (*shaking her head*) No.

**Billy** Tell me what you'll wish first.

**Barbara** Oh, I'll wish that we'll always be happy. And always love each other. What will you wish?

**Billy** Better not tell you.

**Barbara** Why not, pet?

**Billy** You might be cross.

**Barbara** Why would I be cross?

**Billy** Oh, I don't know ... You might think me too ... well, forward. (*He glances at her face but can see no reaction*) Barbara ...? Do you think it's wrong for people to have — you know, feelings?

**Barbara** Not if they're genuinely in love with each other.

**Billy** Like we are.

**Barbara** (*uncertainly*) Yes.

**Billy** Would you think it wrong of me to have — feelings?
**Barbara** (*briskly and firmly*) I think we ought to be married first.
**Billy** (*placing his hand on Barbara's knee*) Darling ...
**Barbara** Are you feeling all right?
**Billy** Of course, darling. Why?
**Barbara** Look where your hand is.
**Billy** Darling, don't you want me to touch you?
**Barbara** (*shrugging*) It seems ... indecent, somehow.
**Billy** Are you feeling all right?
**Barbara** Yes, of course.
**Billy** How do you feel?
**Barbara** Contented.
**Billy** You don't feel ... you know — restless?
**Barbara** No.
**Billy** Finish your drink.
**Barbara** In a minute. (*She opens her handbag and offers it towards him*)
Have an orange.

*Billy, snatching the bag from her, throws it down and oranges spill out across the floor*

**Billy** You and your bloody oranges!
**Barbara** (*remonstratively*) Billy! ... Darling!
**Billy** (*placing his head on her shoulder*) I'm sorry, darling. I've had a terrible
morning.
**Barbara** Why? What's happened?
**Billy** Oh, nothing. The usual. Family and things. Just that I've got a headache.
**Barbara** I'm sorry, pet. You know, you ought to see a doctor.
**Billy** I've seen doctors — specialists — I've seen them all. All they could
give me was a crepe bandage.

*Barbara, unimpressed, licks her fingers*

You know, my darling, I think you have feelings, too. Deep down.
**Barbara** (*examining her hands distastefully*) Oooh, sticky paws!
**Billy** Wipe them on the cushion. (*He rises as a thought strikes him*) You can
go upstairs if you want. Use our bathroom.
**Barbara**, Thank you.

*Barbara, picking up her handbag, crosses into the hall and goes upstairs*

*Billy picks up her glass and crosses to the cocktail cabinet, where he pours
out two more drinks. Taking the "passion pills" from his pocket, he adds two
pills to Barbara's glass and then, on impulse, he adds the entire contents of*

*the bottle into her glass. He is standing admiring the glass and its contents as the telephone rings in the hall. He places the glass on the table and crosses into the hall where he picks up the phone*

**Billy** The Fisher residence? Can I help you? (*His manner changes*) Oh, hullo, Mr Duxbury. No, well, I'm sorry but I've had an accident. I was just leaving for work and I spilt this hot water down my arm. I had to get it bandaged. ... Oh, well, I think there's a very simple explanation for that, Mr Duxbury. You see, there's a lot of those figures that haven't been carried forward. ... I use my own individual system. ... No. No, not me, Mr Duxbury. Well, I'm sure you'll find that there's a very simple explanation. ... What? Monday morning? Yes, of course I'll be there. Prompt. Thank you, Mr Duxbury. Thank you for ringing. Goodbye, then. (*He puts down the telephone for a moment and is lost in depression. He brightens as, in his imagination, he addresses his employer*) Well, look Duxbury — we're not going to argue over trivialities. As soon as I've finalized my arrangements with Mr Boon I'll get in touch with you. (*He picks up the telephone*) Hello, Duxbury? ... I'm afraid the answer is "no". I fully agree that a partnership sounds very attractive — but frankly my interests lie in other directions. I'm quite willing to invest in your business, but I just have not the time to take over the administrative side. ... Oh, I agree that you have a sound proposition there. ... Granted! I take your point, Mr Duxbury. What's that little saying of yours "You've got to come down to earth." It's not a question of coming down to earth, old man. Some of us belong in the stars. The best of luck, Mr Duxbury, and keep writing ...

*He breaks off as*

*Barbara approaches down the stairs*

*For her benefit, he goes into another fantasy as she passes him and enters the living-room*

Well, Doctor, if the leg's got to come off — it's got to come off ... (*He replaces the telephone and looks speculatively at the living-room door*) It's not a question of coming down to earth, Mr Duxbury. (*He pauses*) Some of us, Mr Duxbury, belong in the stars.

*Billy, who has now regained his self-confidence, enters the living-room and crosses towards Barbara with her glass of port*

CURTAIN

# ACT II

*Afternoon of the same day*

*It is late afternoon and just after tea-time in the Fisher household. Alice is moving in and out of the kitchen clearing the tea-things from the living-room table. The best tea-service has been brought out for Barbara's benefit, although Florence has insisted upon having her usual pint-pot. A strange silence has fallen upon the living-room caused partly by Barbara's disclosure that she has recently become engaged to Billy — and partly by Florence's insistence on taking her time over her tea. Florence, in fact, is the only one remaining at the table. Geoffrey has moved away to a chair and Barbara is seated on the couch. Billy is in the hall engaged in a phone conversation and has closed the door to the living-room*

**Billy** ... Rita, will you listen for a minute! ... No, listen to what I'm telling you! The ring's still at the jeweller's! Of course it's all right ... Well, what's the sense in coming round here now! It isn't here — I've just told you, it's at the jeweller's ... Rita! (*He puts down the phone*) Oh blimey! ... (*He takes up the phone and dials a number*)

**Barbara** (*in an attempt to break the silence*) Of course, we haven't fixed the date or anything. (*There is a pause*) We won't be thinking of getting married for quite a while yet.

**Geoffrey** (*a slight pause*) Well, what you going to live on? The pair of you? He'll never have a bloody penny.

**Florence** And there was none of this hire purchase in them days. What you couldn't pay for you didn't have. I don't agree with it. He didn't either. It's only muck and rubbish when it's there.

*Alice returns from the kitchen and fills a tray with used tea-things. She picks up Florence's pint-pot*

I haven't finished with that yet.

*Alice replaces the pot*

*Billy puts down the phone in exasperation. He picks it up and dials another number. Alice returns into the kitchen with the tray*

**Barbara** We had thought of a cottage in Devon.

**Geoffrey** Bloody Devon! He'll never get past the end of our street.

**Florence** She needn't have opened that tin of salmon — it's not been touched hardly.

**Barbara** I don't believe in long engagements — but I don't mind waiting.

**Geoffrey** You'll wait till bloody Domesday if you wait for that sackless article. He's not had a shave yet.

**Alice** (*putting her head round the kitchen door*) Come on, Mother! It's only you we're waiting for.

**Florence** (*mumbling to herself*) She knows I haven't got to be rushed. I don't know what she does it for ...

*An awkward silence falls upon the living-room. Billy speaks into the telephone*

**Billy** Arthur? ... Look, you've got to do something for me. Stop Rita coming round here. ... Well, go round to their house! She's after the ring and Barbara's still got it. ... No, did she heckerslike! I told you they were aspirins. Don't stand there yattering, get your skates on!

*He slams down the receiver*

**Florence** (*who has been mumbling quietly to herself throughout the above now raises her voice to address the sideboard*) It's every tea-time alike. Rush, rush, rush. They've got no consideration. She knows I'm not well.

**Barbara** (*politely*) Billy was saying you'd not been well.

**Geoffrey** Take no notice of what he says — he'll have you as bloody daft as his-self.

*Billy opens the door and enters the living-room*

You'll stand talking on that phone till you look like a bloody telephone. Who was it, then?

**Billy** Only Arthur.

**Geoffrey** What's he bloody want?

**Billy** Oh — nothing.

**Geoffrey** He takes his time asking for it.

**Alice** (*entering from the kitchen*) How's his mother?

**Billy** (*crossing to the fireplace*) All right — considering.

**Barbara** Arthur's mother? Has she been ill?

**Geoffrey** That's the bloody tale he's come home with.

**Billy** (*shuffling awkwardly in front of the fire*) She's been off colour, but she's all right.

**Geoffrey** By, if I don't knock some sense into you! Stand up straight and get your hands out of your pockets! You want to get married, you do!

**Florence** She wants to sew them up. With a needle and cotton. She should sew them up.

**Geoffrey** You'll have to brighten your ideas up, then!

**Florence** A needle and a bit of black cotton. That'd stop him. Then he couldn't put them in his pockets.

**Alice** Mother, haven't you finished that tea yet! Why don't you finish it by the fire. I've got to get cleared up.

**Florence** (*rising and crossing slowly to sit by the fire*) I can't be up and down — up and down — every five minutes. She knows it doesn't do me any good. And that fire's too hot. He banks it up till it's like a furnace in here. I can't be putting up with it.

**Alice** (*clearing the remains off the table*) Well, it's all very well, Mother, I like to get things done. Then it's finished with.

**Barbara** Can I be giving you a hand, Mrs Fisher?

**Alice** It's all right, Barbara. I don't know why our Billy doesn't wash up once in a while.

**Geoffrey** He can't wash his bloody self, never mind the pots.

**Barbara** (*rising and crossing towards the kitchen*) I don't mind.

*Barbara and Alice exit into the kitchen*

*Billy crosses to sit on the couch and Geoffrey rises. There is an embarrassed silence. There is a first attempt at contact between Billy and his father*

**Geoffrey** She doesn't have much to say for herself ... Where do you say she works, then?

**Billy** Turnbull and Mason's.

**Geoffrey** Who?

**Billy** Solicitors. Up Sheepgate.

**Geoffrey** Oh aye?

**Billy** Shorthand-typist.

**Geoffrey** She likes her food, doesn't she? She'll take some keeping. By bloody hell! She had her share of that pork pie, didn't she?

**Billy** She lives up Cragside. On that new estate.

**Geoffrey** She'll need to live up Cragside the way she eats. She can shift them tinned oranges when she starts, can't she? Mind you, she needs it. She's a big lass, isn't she? Big-boned.

**Billy** Yes.

**Geoffrey** (*after a pause*) You're reckoning on getting married then?

**Billy** Thinking about it.

**Geoffrey** You've got your bloody self engaged, anyroad.

**Billy** Yes.

**Geoffrey** So she was saying. You never told us.

**Billy** No. I was meaning to.

**Geoffrey** That was a bit of a daft trick to do, wasn't it?

**Billy** Oh, I don't know.

**Geoffrey** I mean, at your age like. You're only young yet. You re not old enough to start thinking about getting married.

**Billy** There's no hurry.

**Geoffrey** No. But you'll have to put your mind to it sometime.

**Billy** Yes.

**Geoffrey** I mean, you can't go carrying-on the way you've been carrying-on — now, you know. Messing about with different lasses.

**Billy** No — I know. I realize that.

**Geoffrey** You've not only yourself to consider. I don't see why you couldn't have waited a bit. I don't see why you couldn't have told us — your mother and me.

**Billy** I've said — I was meaning to.

**Geoffrey** She's not — you haven't got her into trouble — I mean, there's nothing like that about it, is there?

**Billy** No ... No — 'course not.

*Billy looks across at his father and we feel, for a moment, that they are about to make some point of contact*

**Geoffrey** Well, that's something, anyroad. I suppose she's all right. Just with you not saying anything, that's all.

**Billy** Yes.

**Geoffrey** Only you'll have to start thinking about getting married. Saving up and that.

**Billy** There's plenty of time yet.

**Florence** Well, she didn't touch none of that salmon, I know that. Nobody did. She puts too much out. There's some folk would be glad of that. I tell her ...

*Billy shows some impatience*

**Geoffrey** Course, I don't believe in interfering. You've made your mind up. I don't want you to come to me and say that I stopped you doing it.

**Billy** Well, Dad, it's not that simple. I've not really decided what we'll be doing yet.

**Geoffrey** You couldn't do no worse than us when we started. Me and your mother. We'd nothing — I hadn't two ha'pennies to scratch my backside with. We had to manage.

**Billy** I'm not bothered about managing, Dad. It's just that I hadn't made my mind up.

**Geoffrey** (*almost reverting back to his normal antagonism*) Well, you want to get your bloody mind made up, lad. Right sharp. Before she does it for you.

**Billy** You see ...

**Florence** (*interrupting*) I told her. I had my say. I told her, you don't get married till you're twenty-one.

**Billy** Just a minute, Grandma ...

**Florence** (*ignoring him*) You can do as you like then, I said. Only, I said, don't come running back to me when you can't manage. I said you'll have it to put up with ...

**Billy** (*completely exasperated*) For Christ's sake belt up!

**Geoffrey** (*losing his temper completely*) You what! (*He moves across and grabs Billy by his shirt*) You what did you say? What was that? What did you say?

**Billy** (*frightened but unrepentant*) I merely remarked ...

**Geoffrey** (*shouting*) Talk bloody properly when you talk to me! You were talking different a minute ago, weren't you? What did you just say to your grandma? What did you just say?

*Alice enters from the kitchen*

**Alice** Hey, what's all this row? (*She indicates the kitchen*) Don't you know we've got somebody here?

**Geoffrey** I can't help who's here! She might as well know what he is! Because I'll tell her! (*Shaking him*) He's ignorant! That's what you are, isn't it? Ignorant! Ignorant! Ignorant! Isn't it?

**Alice** Well, don't pull him round. That shirt's clean on.

**Geoffrey** (*releasing his hold on Billy*) I'll clean shirt him before I've finished!

**Alice** Well, what's he done?

**Geoffrey** I'll clean shirt him round his bloody ear-hole. With his bloody fountain pens and his bloody suede shoes! Well, he doesn't go out tonight. I know where he gets it from. He stops in tonight and tomorrow night as well.

**Billy** Look ...

**Geoffrey** Don't "look" me! With your look this and look that! And you can get all that bloody books and rubbish or whatever it is cleared out of that sideboard cupboard as well! Before I chuck 'em out — and you with 'em!

**Billy** What's up? They're not hurting you are they?

*Barbara enters and stands in the kitchen doorway uncertainly*

**Geoffrey** No, and they're not bloody hurting you either!

**Alice** (*quietly*) Well, I don't know what you've done now.

**Geoffrey** Answering back at his grandmother. If that's what they learned him at grammar school I'm glad I'm bloody uneducated! Anyroad, I've finished with him! He knows where there's a suitcase. If he wants to go to London he can bloody well go.

**Alice** (*sharply*) Oh, but he's not.

**Geoffrey** I've finished with him. He can go.

**Alice** Oh, but he's not.

**Geoffrey** He's going! He can get his bloody things together! He's going out!

**Alice** Oh, but he's not. Oh, but he's not. Oh, but he is not!

**Billy** (*trying to get a word in*) Look, can I settle this ...

**Geoffrey** (*interrupting*) It's ever since he started work. Complaining about this and that and the other. If it isn't his boiled eggs it's something else. You have to get special bloody wheatflakes for him because there's a bloody plastic bloody submarine in the packet. Splashing about in the kitchen at his age. He wants putting away. Well, I've had enough — he can go.

**Alice** Oh, but he's not. Now, you just listen to me, Geoffrey. He's not old enough to go to London or anywhere else.

**Geoffrey** He's old enough to get himself engaged. He thinks he is. He's old enough and bloody daft enough.

**Alice** Well, you said yourself. He doesn't think. He gets ideas in his head.

**Geoffrey** He can go. I've finished with him.

**Alice** Oh, but he is not. Not while I'm here.

**Barbara** (*who has been staring at Florence* ) Mrs Fisher ...

**Geoffrey** (*ignoring her*) He wants to get into the bloody army, that's what he wants to do.

**Alice** (*spiritedly*) Yes, and you want to get into the bloody army as well.

**Barbara** Mrs Fisher. I don't think Billy's grandma's very well.

*Alice, Geoffrey and Billy turn and look at Florence who is sitting slumped in her chair.*

**Alice** (*rushing across to her mother*) Now look what you've done!

**Geoffrey** (*to Billy*) I hope you're bloody satisfied now. She's had another do.

**Alice** It's no use blaming him, Geoffrey. You're both as bad as each other. Well, don't just stand there — get me the smelling salts.

**Barbara** (*coming forward*) Can I be doing anything, Mrs Fisher?

**Alice** No ... no, it's all right. She's getting old, that's all. He'll see to it.

**Geoffrey** (*crossing to the sideboard, searching through the drawers*) It's happening too bloody often is this. We can't be having this game every fortnight — neither sense nor reason in it.

**Alice** Well, she can't help it, Geoffrey. It's not her fault.

**Geoffrey** She'll have to see that bloody doctor. If I've to take time off and take her myself — she'll have to see him.

**Alice** She won't see him.

**Geoffrey** It's getting past a joke is this. It's not his fault he's bloody black. (*Rifling through a second drawer*) I wish you'd keep them salts in the same place. Never here when you want them.

**Alice** (*patting her mother's wrists*) Hurry up, Geoffrey!

**Florence** (*who has been slowly coming round during the above begins to mumble*) I told her about that fire. Banking it up. I get too hot and then I go off. They don't think. Rushing me with my tea.

**Alice** It's all right, Mother. You'll be all right.

*Geoffrey locates the bottle of smelling salts*

**Geoffrey** (*crossing and handing them to Alice*) Does she want these bloody salts or not?

**Alice** (*taking the bottle from Geoffrey*) She'd better have them. (*She opens the bottle and holds it under Florence's nose*)

**Florence** Feathers.

**Geoffrey** She's off. She's bloody rambling.

**Florence** She wants to burn some feathers. Never mind salts. I can't be doing with salts. They make me bilious.

**Alice** It's all right, Mother. (*To Geoffrey*) We'd better get her upstairs. She's too hot in here anyway.

**Geoffrey** She'll be too bloody cold if she doesn't see that doctor. It's not fair on us. It's us that has it to put up with.

**Barbara** Shall I fetch you a glass of water?

**Alice** No — she doesn't have water. She'll be all right in a minute.

**Geoffrey** It's happening too regular is this. It's every week alike. And it's always on bloody Saturdays. We can't even sit down to us tea in peace.

**Alice** Don't go on at her — you'll only make her worse. Just help me get her off to bed.

**Geoffrey** (*putting his arm round Florence and raising her to her feet; gruffly compassionate*) Come on then, Mother. Let's be having you. She's a bloody ton weight. She puts some weight on for somebody who never eats nothing. (*To Florence*) You're putting weight on.

**Alice** Don't stand there, Billy. Help your father.

**Geoffrey** (*piloting Florence towards the door*) By bloody hell — don't ask him to do nothing. He'll drop her down the bedroom stairs.

**Alice** (*crossing to help him*) You never give him a chance.

*Alice and Geoffrey support Florence and move off through the hall and up the stairs*

**Florence** They ought to put a bed down here ... Them stairs is too steep ...
**Geoffrey** Now steady ... Steady on, lass ... Plenty of time.

*Florence continues to mumble to herself as they go upstairs. We cannot hear what she is saying but one sentence comes out plainly as they disappear into the bedroom*

**Florence** They could have got the bungalow.

*In the living-room there is an embarrassed silence between Billy and Barbara. Billy absent-mindedly picks up Florence's handbag and looks inside it. He goes through the contents idly and takes out an obsolete ration book*

**Billy** Do you know, she still keeps her old ration book?
**Barbara** I noticed she didn't look very well. Even at tea-time. I noticed but I didn't like to say anything.
**Billy** (*after a pause*) You wouldn't think she'd been all over the world, would you? Paris — Cairo — Vienna.
**Barbara** (*incredulously*) Who? Your grandma?
**Billy** My grandad was in the Diplomatic Corps. Before he had his leg off. He could speak seven languages, you know. They went all over.
**Barbara** (*completely disbelieving him she decides to ignore this statement*) Do you think your mother's going to like me, pet?
**Billy** He was in the French Foreign Legion for nine years.
**Barbara** I think we should get on with each other. It's better when you do — really. When families stick together. Why didn't you tell them we'd got engaged?
**Billy** I was going to. Did you show them the ring?
**Barbara** (*examining the ring*) Of course. I show it to everybody. It's lovely. I won't be completely happy until I've got the other one to go with it.
**Billy** Darling ... (*Taking her hand*) You will always love me, won't you?
**Barbara** You know I will.
**Billy** (*his fingers on the engagement ring*) I still say this ring's too big. Why won't you let me get it altered?
**Barbara** (*pulling her hand away*) I don't think it's too big. Anyway, I want everybody to see it first.
**Billy** Well, don't blame me if you lose it. My mother was saying it was nearly coming off while you were washing up. It'll only take a couple of days. And then it'll be there for ever. (*Romantically*) For ever and ever ...
**Barbara** Sweet ...
**Billy** So go on, then. Give me it. You can have it back on Wednesday.
**Barbara** No, I'll never take it off. Never — never.

**Billy** Give me the cowing ring!
**Barbara** Billy!
**Billy** (*moving away from her in disgust*) Oh, please yourself then. Don't say
I didn't warn you.

*Rita approaches the house through the garden. She is a small girl with
blonde hair — seventeen years old but she dresses to look much older. She
is common and hard and works in a snack bar*

**Barbara** Now you're cross. Don't be, pet. I'll take care of it. And I'll never
lose it.

*Rita rings the bell*

**Billy** Just a minute. (*He crosses into the hall and opens the front door*) Rita!
**Rita** (*moving forward menacingly*) Right, I suppose you ...
**Billy** (*interrupting her*) Just a minute!

*He slams the door on Rita and moves across the hall to speak to Barbara*

Just a minute! (*He closes the living-room door*)

*Alice appears at the top of the staircase*

**Alice** Who is it, Billy?
**Billy** Just a minute!

*Billy opens the front door and enters the garden, closing the door behind him*

*Alice goes back into the bedroom*

*Barbara takes an orange from her handbag and is peeling it as the Lights fade
down on the living-room and the Lights come up on the garden set*

Hallo, Rita.
**Rita** (*her conversation consists mainly of clichés and expressions picked up
on amorous evenings spent with friendly American airmen*) Ooh! Look
what's crawled out of the cheese!
**Billy** Hallo, Rita — sorry I can't ask you in.
**Rita** Get back in the knife-box, big-head.
**Billy** We're flooded. The pipes have burst.
**Rita** Are you kidding? Here, pull the other one — it's got bells on it.
**Billy** What's the matter, darling? Is anything wrong?

**Rita** Hark at Lord Muck. Don't come the innocent with me. You know what's wrong. I thought you were going to your uncle's on Wednesday night.

**Billy** I did go to my uncle's. My Uncle Herbert's.

**Rita** Well, you didn't then — because somebody saw you. Sitting in the Gaumont. With your arm round a lass eating oranges.

**Billy** They didn't see me. I was at my Uncle Ernest's playing Monopoly.

**Rita** (*imitating him*) At my Uncle Ernest's playing Monopoly. You rotten liar! You're just muck. You're rotten, that's what you are. And where's my engagement ring?

**Billy** I'm glad you asked me that question. Because I called into the shop this morning and the man said it might be another week.

**Rita** (*again imitating him*) The man said it might be another week. You're worse than muck. You're rotten.

**Billy** No, because they can't do it up here. They've got to send it to Bradford. They've got three people off ill.

**Rita** (*again imitating him*) Three people off ill. Yes, I suppose they're all having their legs off. To hear you talk everybody's having their leg off. And another thing, I thought I was coming round for my tea this afternoon. To meet your rotten mother.

**Billy** Yes, darling, but something happened. My grandma was taken ill. Last Thursday. They've got her in bed.

**Rita** Well, I am going to see your rotten mother — I'll tell you that. My name's not "Silly", you know. Either you get me that rotten ring back or I'm going to see your rotten mother.

**Billy** (*attempting to quieten her*) Sssh, darling!

**Rita** (*raising her voice*) And your rotten father! And your rotten grandmother!

*In a wild attempt to quieten Rita, Billy takes her in his arms and kisses her. She responds with an automatic animal passion. They break away*

You are rotten to me, Billy. I'm not kidding, you know. I still want that ring back. (*Her voice rises again*) And my dad wants to know where it is as well. We're supposed to be engaged, you know.

**Billy** You once said you didn't want to marry me.

**Rita** Don't come that tale with me. I said I didn't want to live in a rotten cottage in Devon — that's all.

**Billy** We'll live wherever you like, darling. Nothing matters as long as we're together.

**Rita** Well, can you get it back tonight, then?

**Billy** Of course I can, darling. If that's what you want. (*He kisses her again*) Darling, darling, darling.

**Rita** (*pushing Billy away as his hand creeps round her back*) Hey, Bolton
Wanderer! Keep your mucky hands to yourself.
**Billy** Tell me you're not cross with me, darling.
**Rita** (*imitating him*) Tell me you're not cross ... Put another record on, we've
heard that one. And get that ring back.
**Billy** I will. I promise, darling. I'll go down to the shop. I'll give it to you
tonight — at the dance.
**Rita** You'd better do — or else there'll be bother. I wouldn't like to be in your
shoes if my father comes round. And he will, you know. And he won't
stand arguing in the garden.

*Billy kisses her again*

Go on, then. Go in and get your coat on — and get off for that ring.
**Billy** See you tonight, darling.
**Rita** Never mind see you tonight, shops'll be shut in half an hour. You'll get
off now. Go on, then, get your coat. You can walk me down as far as the
bus-stop. Go on, Dateless, don't stand there catching flies.
**Billy** I can't go yet.
**Rita** Why not? What's stopping you?
**Billy** I'm waiting to go to the lavatory. My mam's on.
**Rita** I'll be walking on. You catch me up.

*Rita walks off slowly, down the garden and goes*

*Billy enters the house. As he crosses through the hall the Lights fade down
in the garden and come up in the living-room. Barbara is just finishing eating
the orange*

**Billy** Hey, listen! I've just had my fortune told by a gipsy.
**Barbara** I've eaten a whole orange while I've been waiting.
**Billy** She says there's a curse on me.
**Barbara** Your mother's not come down yet. Neither has your father.
**Billy** I'm going to experience sorrow and misfortune but after a long journey
things will start to go right. Hey, she had a baby on her back like a Red
Indian.
**Barbara** Do you think she'll be all right — your grandmother?

*Billy crosses and sits in the armchair*

**Billy** Who? Oh, my grandma! Yes, she'll be all right. It's just that she's got
this rare disease — they're trying a new drug out on her.

**Barbara** She looked as though she was having some kind of fit at first. I noticed when you were having that row with your father.

**Billy** They've only tried it out three times — this drug. Once on President Eisenhower, then the Duke of Windsor and then my grandma.

**Barbara** Honestly! No wonder your father gets cross with you.

**Billy** How do you mean?

**Barbara** Well, all these stories you keep on telling — no wonder he keeps losing his temper.

**Billy** Oh, you don't take any notice of him.

**Barbara** Billy?

**Billy** What

**Barbara** What was your father saying? About you going to London?

**Billy** Did he? When? I never heard him.

**Barbara** When he was talking about answering back at your grandmother. When he got hold of your shirt. He said, "If you want to go to London you can 'B' well go." He swore.

**Billy** I know. He's been summonsed twice for using bad language.

**Barbara** Yes, but what did he mean?

**Billy** What? About going to London?

**Barbara** Yes.

**Billy** Ah, well — there's a very interesting story behind that.

**Barbara** No, Billy, this is important — to us. You've got to think about me now.

**Billy** (*rising and crossing towards her*) It's for you I'm doing it, my darling.

**Barbara** What do you mean?

**Billy** (*sitting down beside her and taking her hand, he goes off into a fantasy*) Isn't it obvious? How can we go on living like this?

**Barbara** (*automatically freeing her hand, she takes an orange from her handbag*) What do you mean, pet? Like what?

**Billy** In this — this atmosphere. Do you honestly think that we could ever be happy — I mean really happy — here?

**Barbara** Where?

**Billy** In this house. There's the shadow of my father across this house. He's a bitter man, Barbara.

**Barbara** (*settling down and beginning to peel the orange*) Why? What for? What about?

**Billy** He's jealous. Every time he looks at me he sees his own hopes and the failure of his own ambitions.

**Barbara** Your father?

**Billy** He had his dreams once. He can't bear it — seeing me on the brink of success. He was going to be a writer too.

**Barbara** Billy, if this is going to be another of your stories ...

**Billy** You don't have to believe me. The evidence is here — in this house.

**Barbara** Evidence? How do you mean — evidence?
**Billy** (*pointing to the sideboard*) It's all in there.
**Barbara** What is?
**Billy** Go and look for yourself. In that cupboard.

*Barbara rises and crosses to the sideboard. She tugs at the handle on Billy's cupboard*

**Barbara** It's locked.
**Billy** (*meaningly*) Yes.
**Barbara** Where's the key?
**Billy** God knows. I was four years old when that was locked, Barbara. It's never been opened since.
**Barbara** (*crossing towards Billy*) Well, what's supposed to be in it?
**Billy** Hopes! Dreams! Ambitions! The life work of a disillusioned man. Barbara, there must be forty or fifty unpublished novels in that cupboard. All on the same bitter theme.
**Barbara** (*in half-belief*) Well, we can't all be geniuses.
**Billy** Perhaps not. But he crucified himself in the attempt. Sitting night after night at that table. Chewing at his pen. And when the words wouldn't come he'd take it out on us.
**Barbara** But what about going to London? What about our cottage in Devon?

*Alice emerges from the bedroom and comes down the stairs*

**Billy** Well, it's all down south, Barbara. We could live in the New Forest. We could have a cottage there — a woodman's cottage — in a clearing.
**Barbara** I think I'd be frightened. Living in a forest.
**Billy** (*putting his arm round her*) Not with me to look after you, you wouldn't.

*Billy rises awkwardly as Alice enters the room. Alice is faintly preoccupied. She crosses towards the kitchen and speaks almost to herself*

**Alice** Well, she seems to be resting.

*Alice goes into the kitchen. There is a slight feeling of embarrassment between Billy and Barbara and then Barbara speaks to break the silence*

**Barbara** Are we going out dancing tonight?
**Billy** If you like ... (*He claps his hand to his forehead in an over-dramatic gesture*) Oh, no! Just remembered!

**Barbara** (*suspiciously*) What?

**Billy** I promised to go round to my Uncle Herbert's tonight. To play Monopoly. It's his birthday.

**Barbara** Funny you never told me before. You're always having to go round to your Uncle Herbert's. Anyway, I thought it was your Uncle Ernest who played Monopoly?

**Billy** Ah, well ... I'm glad you asked me that question. You see, my Uncle Herbert ...

**Barbara** (*interrupting*) Oh, don't bother. You and your relatives. If I didn't know you better I'd think you had another girl.

**Billy** Darling! What a thing to say!

**Barbara** You know that Liz is back in town, don't you?

**Billy** Liz who?

**Barbara** You know who. That dirty girl. I'm surprised you weren't ashamed to be seen with her.

**Billy** Oh, her ... I haven't seen her for donkey's years.

*Alice enters from the kitchen. She is carrying a tumbler containing a white liquid which she is stirring with a spoon*

**Alice** Her breathing's all right — she's still awake, though. I think she'd be better if we could get her off to sleep.

**Barbara** She was looking tired this afternoon.

**Alice** (*gently reprimanding*) Well, I blame you as much as anybody. You set your father off and then it sets her off. I've told you time and time again.

**Billy** (*half ashamed*) She's all right now, is she, then?

**Alice** Is she ever all right?

**Barbara** Are you quite sure there's nothing I can do? Could she eat an orange?

**Alice** I'm going to get the doctor in to her — be on the safe side. Whether she wants him or not. Your father's sitting with her. (*She hands him the tumbler*) Can you take this up without spilling it?

**Billy** (*taking the tumbler reluctantly*) Who? Me?

**Alice** Either that or ring the doctor up for me. (*Rather impatiently*) But do something, lad, don't just stand there.

*Alice turns away from him and walks briskly into the hall where she picks up the phone. Billy stands indecisively for a moment and then crosses through into the hall and up the stairs as Alice dials the number. She waits for a reply and glances up at Billy who has, for no reason at all, developed a limp*

(*Calling up to him*) Now, what are you playing at!

*Billy stops limping and quickens his pace and goes into the bedroom*

(*Turning back to the phone*) Hallo, is that the surgery? ... Well, it's Mrs Fisher, forty-two Park Drive. ... Yes, that's right. Only it's my mother again. Mrs Boothroyd. Do you think the doctor could call round? ... Oh, dear. Only we've got her in bed again ... I've given her her tablets — and the mixture. ... Well, will you ask him to come round as soon as he can? ... Yes, yes, I will, I will — thank you very much. Goodbye. (*She replaces the phone and crosses into the living-room*) You don't like to bother them on a Saturday but what else can you do?

**Barbara** Is the doctor coming, Mrs Fisher?

**Alice** He's coming sometime — when he's ready. It'll be nine o'clock again, I suppose. He's already out on his calls.

**Barbara** I shouldn't worry. He'll be round as soon as he can.

**Alice** (*sitting*) You can't help worrying sometimes. If I don't worry nobody else will. It's just getting me down, is this. It's just one thing after another.

**Barbara** (*returning to her seat on the couch and taking up the orange*) Would you like a piece of orange, Mrs Fisher?

*Alice looks up and, for the first time, realizes that Barbara is trying to help*

**Alice** No. No, thank you. Not just at this minute, love. Thank you.

**Barbara** Would it be better if I went? (*Half rising*) I mean if I'm in the way.

**Alice** No, don't be silly. You sit yourself down. I'm only sorry it's happened while you were here.

**Barbara** (*returning to her seat*) You can't arrange illnesses, can you?

**Alice** You can't. I only wish you could. Only she has these turns and all you can do is put her to bed. But she always seems to pick the most awkward times. Still, you can't blame her. It's not her fault. You might think it is to hear him talk. You'd think she does it on purpose, to listen to him.

**Barbara** She might be better before the doctor comes.

**Alice** It wears me out, I know that. And if it isn't her it's our Billy. I don't know what we're going to do with him.

**Barbara** I think he wants to help — but he doesn't like to offer.

**Alice** He didn't used to be like this. He's got to grow up sometime. I don't know, it might be better if he did go to London. It might put some sense into him if he had to look after himself.

**Barbara** Well, that's what I don't understand, Mrs Fisher. Is he going to London?

**Alice** Well, he reckons he is. Hasn't he said anything to you?

**Barbara** Well, not really. I only heard what his father said. I tried to ask him.

**Alice** What did he say to you?

**Barbara** Nothing, really. (*She indicates the sideboard*) He just started talking about that cupboard.

**Alice** Oh, don't talk to me about that cupboard. I don't know what he keeps in there. I'm frightened to ask, to tell you the honest truth.

**Barbara** He said it had been locked since he was four years old.

**Alice** I don't know why he says these things. I mean, what good does it do him? It's not as if he gets anything out of it.

**Barbara** I'm sure I don't know. He told me Mr Fisher was a captain on a petrol ship.

**Alice** Don't let his father hear you say that — else there'll be trouble. He'll murder him one of these days. If he knew all I know he'd have murdered him long ago. I could do it myself sometimes. And he says things we can find out about, that's what I don't understand. He told me that young lad who works in the fruit shop had gassed himself — and he knows I go in there every Tuesday.

**Barbara** I know. He says all kinds of things.

**Alice** I don't know where he'll end up — it's not our fault, I do know that. We've done our best for him. His father says it's since he started work — but I know different. It's ever since he went to that grammar school. He wanted to go, so we let him — he'd not been there five minutes before he wanted to leave. And we had it all to pay for, you know — he never appreciated it. School uniform, he loses his cap first week. Cricketing trousers, he never wore them. We bought him a satchel and he let a lad run away with it. Then there was his books to pay for — well, he never reads them. It's just been a waste of time and money. You'd think he'd been dragged up. He's not cleaned his shoes for six months.

**Barbara** I tell him about his shoes. He takes no notice. And his hair — he won't have a haircut, will he?

**Alice** Well, he doesn't take after me — or his father. And it's us that's got to clean up after him. He got them suede shoes so he wouldn't have to bother cleaning them — but you can't just not touch them. He trod in some dog-dirt on Tuesday and — do you know? — he walked it round this house for three days. I had to get a knife and scrape it off myself in the finish. (*Distastefully, recalling the incident*) Pooh! You could smell it all over the house.

**Barbara** My mother won't have a dog. And she hates cats.

**Alice** You can't keep on telling him — it just goes in one ear and out the other. He wants watching all the time, that's his trouble. You see, if he'd gone into the business with his father, like we wanted him to, we could have kept an eye on him more. But he won't listen. He went after all kinds of daft jobs. That lady in the Juvenile Employment Bureau, she lost patience with him. He wouldn't have this and he wouldn't have that. And she offered him some lovely jobs to begin with. He could have gone as a junior trainee at the Co-op Bank if he'd wanted to. She offered him that.

**Barbara** I know somebody who works there, she likes it. They've got their own social club.

**Alice** She just stopped bothering. She couldn't get any sense out of him. She asked him what he did want in the end and he told her he wanted to be either a merchant seaman or a concert pianist. Grammar school! You'd think he'd been to the Silly School. He shows me up.

**Barbara** How did he come to work for Shadrack and Duxbury's?

**Alice** Don't ask me. He'd been left school a fortnight and he was still no nearer a job — he wanted to work in the museum by this time. We were sick and tired of having him lounging about the house. His father comes home one morning at twelve o'clock and finds him playing with some Plasticine. He went mad. He told him straight out. He says, you get out of this house and get yourself a job, my lad, he says. And, he says, don't you dare come back without one — or I'll knock your blooming head right off your shoulders — only he didn't say blooming.

**Barbara** No, I can imagine.

**Alice** So, of course, our Billy goes out and waltzes back two hours later and says he's working for an undertaker — start on Monday. He's been there ever since.

**Barbara** I don't think he likes it, though, does he?

**Alice** Like it or lump it, he's got to work for his living. Never mind going to London. He's got no mind of his own, that's his trouble. He listens to these pals he's got. What they do he's got to do. I'm only glad he's found himself a sensible lass, for once.

*Billy emerges from the bedroom and comes down the stairs*

**Barbara** I think it was that girl he used to go about with before he met me, Mrs Fisher. That funny girl. That Liz. She used to put a lot of ideas into his head.

*Billy pauses at the foot of the stairs and listens to their conversation*

**Alice** Oh, that one. I've seen him with her. She looked as though a good bath wouldn't do her any harm. I don't know what kind of a family she comes from. I'm only glad she's gone.

**Barbara** She's come back again, didn't you know? She goes off all over, all the time. By herself. I don't think she's got any family. Do you know what I don't like about her, Mrs Fisher? She smokes and she keeps her cigarette in her mouth when she's talking. I could never do that. It looks common.

**Alice** You could always tell when he'd been out with her. The ideas he used to come home with. He comes home one night and says he wants to go off on holiday with her. To the Norfolk Broads, if you like. I told him — straight. I said, that's not the way we do things in this house. I said, if you want to go on holiday you can come to Morecambe with us — and if you don't you can stop at home.

**Barbara** I don't believe in mixed holidays — not before you're married.
**Alice** I'm sure you don't, love. You wouldn't be sitting here if you did, I can tell you.
**Barbara** He was saying you wouldn't mind if I went to Blackpool with him for a week — but I wouldn't. I don't believe in anything like that.
**Alice** He was saying what!
**Billy** (*entering hastily and changing the subject*) Hey, listen!

*Alice and Barbara turn to Billy who is trying to think of something to say next*

(*He tries to joke in desperation*) Fifteen men under one umbrella and not one of them got wet. (*He evokes no reaction*) It wasn't raining.
**Alice** (*to Barbara*) Well, you can't say you don't know what you're letting yourself in for. (*To Billy*) Stop acting so daft with people poorly. We've got enough on our plates without you.
**Barbara** How's your grandma, Billy? Is she any better?
**Alice** Has she gone off to sleep yet?
**Billy** She looks all right to me.
**Alice** Is your father all right with her? Would he like me to go up? Does he want anything?
**Billy** I don't know.
**Alice** No, and I don't suppose you care. (*Losing her temper*) Have you had a wash since you got up this morning?
**Billy** Course I have.
**Alice** Yes, a cat-lick. I bet you didn't take your shirt off, did you? You'll have to smarten your ideas up, you know, if you want to go script-writing. They don't have them on the B.B.C. with mucky necks. You'll start washing your own shirts in future, I can't get them clean.
**Billy** (*acutely embarrassed but, for Barbara's benefit, he pretends to be amused and winds an imaginary gramophone handle*) Crikey Moses, she's off!
**Barbara** Well, you can't say you've had a shave this morning, Billy because you haven't.
**Billy** I'm growing a beard, if you want to know.
**Alice** Oh no, you're not. We're having no beards in this house.
**Barbara** I don't think I'd like you with a beard, Billy.
**Alice** He's not having a beard.
**Billy** I'm having a bloody beard.
**Alice** Hey, hey, hey! Language! Don't you start coming out with that talk! Else you'll get a shock coming, big as you are! We get enough of that from your father.
**Billy** Well, I'm still having a beard. I can grow one in six weeks.

**Barbara** I don't think you should, Billy. Not if your mother doesn't want you to.

**Alice** He's got no say in the matter. If I say he doesn't grow a beard, he doesn't grow one.

**Billy** What's up with you? It's my stinking face!

**Alice** I'll not tell you again about that language! You can start to alter yourself, that's what you can do, my lad. We're not going on like this for much longer. Either brighten your ideas up or do as your father says — and get off to London or where you like. Because we're not going on like this, day in and day out! It's not fair on nobody!

**Billy** Oh, shut up!

**Alice** And you can start watching what you say to people, as well. What did you say to me about that lad in the fruit shop? Gassing himself? And what have you been telling Barbara about that cupboard?

**Billy** What cupboard?

**Alice** You know very well what cupboard!

**Billy** I don't know what cupboard. How do you mean — cupboard?

**Barbara** Your sideboard cupboard.

**Billy** What about it?

**Barbara** That evidence you were talking about. In the cupboard. When you were four years old. All these unpublished novels. Where your father was chewing his pen up.

**Billy** Oh, that! Oh, you should have said. No, you're getting mixed up. I was talking about his invoices that he writes out. He keeps them in that vase — I didn't say anything about any cupboard.

**Barbara** (*shocked*) Billy Fisher! I don't know how you can stand there! He'll be struck down dead one of these days.

**Billy** (*with a pretence at innocence*) What's up?

**Alice** He can stand there as if butter wouldn't melt in his mouth.

**Billy** I don't know what you're all on about.

**Barbara** Oh yes, you do. Don't try and make it out as if it's me, Billy.

**Billy** It is you. Look — Barbara — you were sitting over there, weren't you? On that couch. Because you were eating an orange. And I was standing over there. Right? It is right, isn't it? You were sitting there and I was standing there.

**Barbara** Yes, but then you said your father...

**Alice** Never mind what he said, love, I know what he is.

*Rita enters the garden and stands, for a moment, hesitantly outside the front door*

**Billy** Yes, you'll believe her, won't you?

**Alice** I'd believe anybody before you, Billy I'm very sorry, but there it is. I'd
believe Hitler before I'd believe you.

**Billy** Why don't you come straight out and call me a liar, then!

**Alice** Well, you are one. I don't care who knows it.

**Billy** Well, that's a nice thing for a mother to say, isn't it?

**Alice** Yes, and you're a nice son for a mother to have, aren't you? You don't
think what you're doing to me, do you? You never consider anybody
except yourself.

**Billy** I suppose you do, don't you?

**Alice** Yes, I do. I worry about you, I know that.

**Billy** Well, what about me? Don't you think I worry? I worry about the H-
bomb. You didn't know I nearly went on the Aldermaston march last
Easter, did you? I don't want another war, you know. And what about all
them refugees? You never stop to consider them, do you? Or South Africa.

*At which point Rita makes up her mind, and, without knocking, marches into
the house and into the living-room*

Do you know, Barbara, if you were black and we lived in South Africa I'd
be in gaol by now? Doing fifteen years. (*At which point he breaks off as Rita
makes her entrance*) Hallo, Rita.

**Rita** (*to Billy, indicating Alice*) It takes her some time to come out of the
lavatory, doesn't it? What's she been doing? Writing her will out?

**Alice** (*outraged*) Do you usually come into people's houses without
knocking?

**Rita** I do when people have got my private property. (*To Billy*) Come on —
give.

**Billy** Rita, I don't think you've ever met my mother, have you?

**Rita** No, but she'll know me again, won't she? Come, you and your
stinking rotten jewellers. I'm not daft, you know.

**Alice** (*shocked*) We're not having this! Where does she think she is?

**Billy** (*attempting to guide Rita towards the door, he takes her elbow*) I'll just
take Rita as far as the bus stop, Mother.

**Rita** (*shrugging him away*) Take your mucky hands off me, you rotten
toffee-nosed get. You didn't think I'd come in, did you?

**Alice** No, but I think you'll go out, young lady. And if you've anything to
say to my son you'd better just remember where you are.

**Billy** Well, I'm very glad you have come, Rita, because I feel I owe you a
word of explanation.

**Rita** (*imitating him*) Oooh, I feel I owe you a word of explanation. Get back
in the cheese, with the other maggots.

**Alice** I'm not putting up with this — I shall bring his father down.

**Rita** You can bring his rotten father down. I hope you do. And his rotten grandma.

**Barbara** Billy's grandma, for your information, happens to be ill in bed.

**Rita** (*turning to Barbara for the first time*) Oooh, look what the cat's brought in. Get Madam Fancy-knickers. I suppose this is your rotten sister. I thought she was supposed to be in a rotten iron lung.

**Barbara** For your information, I happen to be Billy's fiancée.

**Rita** (*imitating Barbara*) Oooh, for your information. Well, for your information, he happens to be engaged to me. In front of a witness.

**Billy** How do you mean? What's witnesses got to do with it?

**Barbara** Billy, will you kindly tell me who this girl is?

**Rita** (*imitating her*) Oooh, Billy, will you kindly tell me? Aw, go take a long walk on a short pier, you squint-eyed sow, you're nothing else.

**Alice** Barbara, would you kindly go upstairs and ask Mr Fisher to come down for a minute?

**Rita** You can fetch him down. Fetch all the rotten lot down. You can fetch the cowing iron lung down as well, for all I care.

**Alice** I've never been spoken to like this in all my days.

**Barbara** Shall I go up, Mrs Fisher?

**Rita** (*imitating her*) Oooh, shall I go up, Mrs Fisher? If you can get up the stairs with them bow legs, you can.

**Alice** It's all right, Barbara. I'll deal with this young madam. I've met her type before.

**Billy** I think I can explain all this.

**Barbara** Yes, I think you've got some explaining to do, Billy.

**Rita** He can explain until he's blue in the rotten face. It makes no difference to me.

**Alice** If I knew your mother, young lady, wouldn't I have something to say to her.

**Rita** You can keep out of this. It's between me and him. (*To Billy*) Where's my ring? Has she got it?

*Barbara's right hand instinctively goes to her left*

She has, hasn't she? You've given it to her, haven't you?

**Billy** Ah, well — yes, but you see ... Only there's been a bit of a mix-up. You see, I thought Barbara had broken the engagement off.

**Barbara** Billy!

**Rita** Yeh, well you've got another think coming if you think I'm as daft as she is. You gave that ring to me. And don't think you can go crawling out of it, 'cause you can't. You seem to forget I've got a witness, you know. I've got two. 'Cause Shirley Mitchem saw you giving me it, as well — so you needn't think she didn't. I can go down to the Town Hall, you know.

**Alice**  Now, don't you come running in here with them tales, my girl. You know as well as I do he's under-age.

**Rita**  Ask him if he was under-age down at Foley Bottoms last night. 'Cause I'm not carrying the can back for nobody. He wasn't under-age then. He was over-age more like.

**Alice**  Get out! Get out of my house!

**Barbara**  Have you been untrue to me, Billy? I've got to know.

**Rita**  (*imitating her*) Oooh, have you been untrue to me, Billy! Get out of your pushchair, babyface. (*To Billy*) You're just rotten, aren't you? You are — you're rotten, all through. I've met some people in my time, but of all the lying, scheming ... anyway, you gave that ring to me.

**Billy**  Yes, but, look, Rita ...

**Rita**  (*interrupting*) Don't talk to me, you rotten get. Well, she can have you — if she knows what to do with you, which I very much doubt. You rotten lying get. Garr — you think you're somebody, don't you? But you're nobody. You miserable lying rotten stinking get.

**Billy**  Does this mean you're breaking off our engagement?

**Rita**  You don't get out of it like that. I want that ring.

**Barbara**  (*finding the right word at last*) Billy, have you been — having relations with this girl?

**Rita**  (*swinging round on Barbara* ) What do you think he's been doing? Knitting a pullover? You know what you can do, don't you? You can give me that ring. Because it's mine.

**Alice**  If you don't stop it this minute! (*To Billy*) As for you, I hope you know what you've done, because I don't.

**Rita**  Are you going to give me that ring?

**Barbara**  I shall give the ring back to Billy — if and when I break off the engagement.

**Billy**  (*moving towards her*) Barbara.

**Rita**  Yes, you can go to her. She can have you. And she knows what she can do, the squint-eyed, bow-legged, spotty, snotty-nosed streak of nothing.

**Barbara**  And you know what you can do as well. You can wash your mouth out with soap and water.

**Rita**  (*imitating*) Oooh, you can wash your mouth out with soap and water. You could do with some soap in your ears, you've got carrots growing out of them. Well, you can give me that ring. Before I come over there and get it.

**Alice**  You can get out of this house. I won't tell you again.

**Rita**  Save your breath for blowing out candles. I want my ring. (*Crossing towards Barbara*) Yes, and I'm going to get it.

**Alice**  Get out of my house! Get out! Get out!

*Geoffrey Fisher emerges from the bedroom and comes slowly down the stairs*

**Rita** (*moving right up to Barbara*) Are you going to give me that ring, or aren't you?

**Geoffrey** (*halfway down the stairs*) Mother! ... Mother!

**Rita** Because you'll be in *Emergency Ward Ten* if I don't get it — right sharpish.

**Barbara** Don't you threaten me.

**Rita** I won't threaten you — I'll flatten you! Give me that cowing ring back! (*She makes a grab for Barbara's hand*)

**Barbara** (*pushing her away*) I won't ... I won t ...

**Alice** Will you stop it, the pair of you!

*Geoffrey enters the room and stands in the doorway. He appears not to comprehend what is happening*

**Geoffrey** Mother!

*Geoffrey's word silences Alice, Billy and Barbara who turn and look at him*

**Rita** (*unconcerned*) Give me the ring!

**Geoffrey** You'd better come upstairs. Come now. I think she's dead.

CURTAIN

# ACT III

*Later the same evening*

*It is about half-past nine and quite dark in the garden outside the Fishers'
house. When the action of the play takes place in the garden, however, a street
lamp comes up from the road beyond the garden and off stage. There is also
a small light in the porch of the house. As the* CURTAIN *rises Geoffrey Fisher
is going through the contents of Billy's cupboard which are, at the moment,
spread across the floor of the living-room by the sideboard. Alice Fisher is
sitting in a chair by the fire. She is obviously distraught by the death of her
mother. Geoffrey rummages through the envelopes and papers and then
rises, shaking his head*

**Geoffrey** Well, I can't bloody find it. It's not in here, anyway. He hasn't got
it. It's about the only bloody thing he hasn't got.

**Alice** She might not have had one, Geoffrey — you know what she was like.

**Geoffrey** (*although he hasn't changed his vocabulary there is a more tender
note than usual in his voice*) Don't talk so bloody wet, lass. Everybody's
got a birth certificate.

**Alice** Well, you don't know, Geoffrey, they might not have had them in those
days. She was getting on.

**Geoffrey** Everybody's got a bloody birth certificate. They've had them since
the year dot. If he's got it squat somewhere I'll bloody mark him for life.

**Alice** You can't blame our Billy for everything, Geoffrey. What would he
want with it?

**Geoffrey** (*indicating the papers on the floor*) What's he want with this
bloody lot? There's neither sense nor bloody reason in him. And where is
he, anyway? Where's he taken himself off to?

**Alice** I don't know, Geoffrey. I've given up caring.

**Geoffrey** You'd think he could stay in one bloody night of the year. He ought
to be in tonight. He ought to be in looking after his mother. He's got no
sense of bloody responsibility, that's his trouble.

**Alice** Well, she liked her cup of tea. We'll have that pint-pot to put away now.
She's used that pint-pot for as long as I can remember.

**Geoffrey** She liked her bloody tea, there's no getting away from it. (*He half-
jokes in an attempt to lift Alice out of her depression*) If I had a shilling for
every pot of tea she's supped I'd be a rich man today. Well, there's one good
thing to be said for it, when does the dustbin man come around? 'Cause he
can take all them tins of condensed milk out of her bedroom.

**Alice** We can't throw them away. Somebody might be glad of them. We could send them round to the Old People's Home, or something.

**Geoffrey** Get away with you, you'd poison the bloody lot of them. That stuff doesn't keep for ever you know. They'll be green mouldy.

**Alice** I thought it was supposed to keep — condensed milk.

**Geoffrey** It won't keep twenty bloody years, I'm sure. She's had that pile of tins stacked up there since nineteen thirty-nine. And there's not one of them been opened — not one.

**Alice** Well, they went scarce, Geoffrey, when the war started, you know. That's why she started saving them.

**Geoffrey** Went scarce? Too bloody true they went scarce, she had them all. She hoarded them — she was like a squirrel with them. If Lord Woolton had heard about her in nineteen forty-one she'd have got fifteen years. By bloody hell, she would. (*He reminisces gently*) Hey! I say! Do you remember how I used to pull her leg about it? How I used to tell her the food office was ringing up for her? You couldn't get her near that bloody telephone. She used to let it ring when we were out — she must have lost me pounds.

**Alice** (*not cheered by Geoffrey's attempt at humour*) Well, I only hope you manage as well when you're as old as she was. She's not had an easy life — I wish I could have made it easier for her. She had all us to bring up, you know. And that took some doing.

**Geoffrey** No — she didn't do too bad, to say. What was she? Eighty — what?

**Alice** She'd have been eighty-three in August. Either eighty-three or eighty-two. She didn't seem to know herself.

**Geoffrey** Well, I shan't grumble if I last as long — she had a fair old crack of the whip.

**Alice** She didn't suffer, that's something to be grateful for. Some of them hang on for months and months. What did you say she was talking about? Before she went?

**Geoffrey** Don't ask me. I couldn't hear for that bloody shambles that was going on down here. I've never heard anything like it in all my born days.

**Alice** Well, you can blame our Billy for that, because I do. I've not finished with that Rita-whatever-her-name-is. I shall find out where she lives. I shall go round and I shall find out.

**Geoffrey** I know her. She works in that milk-bar in Sheepgate. I know her and I know her bloody father as well. You know him. Him that's always racing that whippet on the moor. Him with them tattoos all up his arms. Supposed to work in the market, when he does work. They live in them terrace-houses. Down Mill Lane.

**Alice** Well, I shall go round. I shall go round and see her mother.

**Geoffrey** You'll go bloody nowhere. You keep away. We've got enough to cope with without getting mixed up with that lot.

**Alice** I only wish she could have been spared it. If you can't die in peace, what can you do?

**Geoffrey** You don't want to go fretting yourself about that. She heard nothing about it. She was miles away.

**Alice** And what do you say she said? Did she know you?

**Geoffrey** Well, she did at first. She was all right after you went down. And she was all right when our Billy came up with her medicine. She took that all right and kept it down. She was just ramblin' on — like she does. She was chuntering on about a tin of salmon going to waste. Then something about getting her pension book changed at the post office next week. She never knew, you see. It was just this last five minutes when she started to slaver. I was holding her up in bed and she just slumped forward. I thought she was having a bloody fit. But no — she just gave a little jerk with her head — like that. Then she started to slaver. She was just like a baby, Alice. Just like a baby, slavering and gasping for breath. She wet my handkerchief through, I know that. Then she sits straight up — by herself — and says, "Where's my Jack?" I had to think who she was talking about. Then I remember she must have meant your father. Only she always used to call him John, didn't she?

**Alice** (*half to herself*) She hardly ever called him Jack.

**Geoffrey** Then she said, "I love you, Jack". Oh, and before she said, "What are you thinking about?" — she must have been talking to your father, she couldn't have been talking to anyone else. But you had to listen close to, to hear what she was saying. She could hardly speak. By the time she went she couldn't speak at all. She was just slavering.

*There is a pause*

**Alice** You should have called me.

**Geoffrey** (*suddenly compassionate*) She wouldn't have known you. And you wouldn't have liked to have seen her like that. You couldn't have done anything for her — nobody could.

**Alice** You should have called me, Geoffrey.

**Geoffrey** I didn't think it would have done you any good to see her, that's all. (*Reverting to his normal tones*) And, listen! If he thinks he's going to the funeral in them bloody suede shoes, he's got another think coming. There'll be all them Masonics coming — I'm not having him showing me up. He'll get some bloody black ones or stop at home.

**Alice** He's got some black ones but he won't wear them.

**Geoffrey** Well, make him. And think on and see that he gets a bloody good wash on Tuesday morning. When did he have a bath last?

**Alice** Well, there'll be no baths on Tuesday, 'cause I'm not lighting any fires — I shall be too busy. And I still know nothing about the funeral. I wish I'd have seen Mr Duxbury.

**Geoffrey** You only just missed him. If you'd have gone to your Emily's five minutes later you would have seen him. Anyway, they're doing everything. Shadrack and Duxbury's. He says they'll fix the tea for us — the lot.

**Alice** And you still haven't told me what Mr Duxbury said about our Billy — about him getting into bother at work.

**Geoffrey** Don't talk to me about our Billy. I'm going to start putting him in the coal cellar when people come. Duxbury comes to the door — I take him straight upstairs. He starts measuring her up so I left him to it. Come down here and walk into the living-room and there's bloody Dopey sat in here. He's let the fire go out. Kettle boiling its bloody head off. He's sitting with his shoes and socks off and all muck between his toes watching bloody Noddy on television. (*Losing his temper*) His grandmother bloody dead upstairs and all he can do is watch Noddy.

**Alice** I can't understand him. He doesn't seem to have any feeling for anybody.

**Geoffrey** I told him. I said to him, "What are you bloody doing? Do you know Mr Duxbury's upstairs?" He was out of that chair and through that door like a shot. I watched him out of our bedroom window — putting his shoes and socks on in the street. I'll bloody swing for him before I've finished, I will.

**Alice** Well, what did Mr Duxbury say about him?

**Geoffrey** He wasn't going to say anything. Not today. Until I asked him if our Billy had rung up and asked for his cards, like he said he was. Then the lot came out. (*He indicates the calendars*) There's all these calendars he's supposed to have posted, for one. Then there's his petty cash — that doesn't add up. Then there's his postage book. Two pound ten postage money he's had. And he's supposed to have pinched a brass plate off a coffin. What does he want to do a bloody trick like that for?

**Alice** You didn't say anything about postage money before — you just said petty cash.

**Geoffrey** I don't know. Don't ask me. The whole bloody lot's wrong from start to finish. He can't keep his hands off nothing.

**Alice** But what did he say about not taking him to court?

**Geoffrey** How many more bloody times? He says if he stays on — and does his work right, and pays this money back — and stops giving back-chat every five minutes — he'll hear no more about it.

**Alice** But what about him going to London?

**Geoffrey** How the bloody hell can he go to London? He'll go to Dartmoor if he's not careful. He's to stop on there until he's paid this money back — and I know I'm not paying it, if he goes down on his bended knees I'm not paying it.

**Alice** It's a mystery to me why he wanted to take that money in the first place. He never buys anything — and if he does go short he knows he's only to come to me.

**Geoffrey** You've been too soft with him, that's been the bloody trouble, all along. Anyway, you know what he's spent it on, don't you? That bloody engagement ring. That's where the money's gone. Well, he can get that back to the shop for a start. And he can get engaged when he's twenty-one and not before. And he brings no more bloody lasses round here. And he comes in at nine o'clock in future — never mind half-past eleven. There's going to be some changes in this house.

**Alice** Yes, and you've said that before and it's made no difference. He used to get on her nerves.

**Geoffrey** Well, she's not got him to put up with any more. He used to lead her a dog's life. I've seen him — mocking her. And where is he? He's got no bloody right to be out.

**Alice** I don't know where he's got to.

**Geoffrey** He'll know where he's got to when he rolls in here. He'll go straight out again — through the bloody window.

**Alice** We don't want any more rows tonight, Geoffrey. My nerves won't stand it. You've had one row today and you saw what happened. She was all right till you started on our Billy.

**Geoffrey** Don't start bloody blaming me for it. For God's sake. I told her often enough to go to see that doctor.

**Alice** You know very well why she wouldn't go.

**Geoffrey** It was your bloody job to see that she did. I'm not on tap twenty-four hours a bloody day. I've got work to do.

*They are building up to an argument*

**Alice** And I've got my work to do as well. I did my best. I tried to make her go. You know why it was. It was because he was black.

**Geoffrey** I don't care if he was sky-blue bloody pink with yellow dots on. You should have gone with her.

**Alice** (*almost in tears*) It was only this afternoon she was sitting in that chair with a pot of tea. You can say what you like, she was all right till you started on to our Billy.

**Geoffrey** She was never all right. She hadn't been all right for bloody months.

**Alice** It's tomorrow morning I'm thinking about. When I should be taking her up her pot of tea and a Marie Louise biscuit.

**Geoffrey** Will you shut up about bloody pots of tea! You won't fetch her back with pots of bloody tea. She'll get no pots of tea where she's gone.

**Alice** Well, I like to think she will! (*She rises and crosses towards the kitchen*)

**Geoffrey** Where are you going now?

**Alice** I'm going to make myself one.

**Geoffrey**  Sit you down. I'll see to it.
**Alice**  No. No. I'm better when I'm doing something. I'd rather be occupied.

*Alice goes into the kitchen*

**Geoffrey**  (*crossing to join her*) I'll give you a hand, anyway.

*Geoffrey goes into the kitchen as the Lights fade down in the living-room. The Lights come up in the garden — both from the porch and the street lamp. We discover Billy sitting on the garden seat, rather cold and his hands dug deep in his pockets. He lights a cigarette, then rises and crosses to the front door where he listens for a moment through the letter box. Hearing nothing he returns towards the garden seat and sits disconsolately*

*Billy hums to himself and then turns on the seat and takes up a garden cane. He toys with the cane for a moment, attempting to balance it on his fingers. His humming grows louder and he stands and conducts an imaginary orchestra using the cane as a baton. He is humming a military march and he suddenly breaks off as the garden cane becomes, in his imagination, a rifle. He shoulders the cane and marches briskly up and down the garden path*

**Billy**  (*marching*) Lef', ri', lef', ri', lef'-ri'-lef'! Halt! (*He halts*) Order arms! (*He brings the cane down to the "Order" position. He pauses for a moment and the garden cane becomes, in his imagination, an officer's baton which he tucks under his arm and then he marches smartly off to an imaginary saluting base a few paces away. He has become, in his imagination, a major-general*) Dearly beloved Officers and Gentlemen of the Desert Shock Troops. We are assembled at the grave-side here this evening to pay our respects to a great lady. There are many of us here tonight who would not be alive now but for her tender mercies although in her later years she was limbless from the waist down. She struggled valiantly to combat ignorance and disease. Although she will be remembered by the world as the inventor of penicillin and radium we, of this proud regiment, will remember her as our friend — the Lady of the Lamp. I call upon you all to join with me in observing two minutes' silence. (*He removes an imaginary hat which he places under his arm. He lowers his head respectfully and stands in silence. Imitating a bugle he hums the "Last Post"*)

*He is still standing, his head lowered, as Arthur and Liz enter the garden*

*Although Liz is about the same age as Barbara and Rita she has more maturity and self-possession. Although she is dressed casually and is, in fact, wearing the black skirt we have heard so much about, she is not as scruffy as we have been led to believe. She is also wearing a white blouse and a green suede jacket. She is not particularly pretty but is obviously a girl of strong personality. Liz is the only girl for whom Billy has any real feelings. Liz and Arthur stand for a moment looking at Billy, who has not noticed them*

**Arthur**  What's up with him, then?

**Billy**  (*startled and embarrassed*) I didn't hear you coming ... (*He sees Liz for the first time and is even more embarrassed*) Liz.

**Liz**  Hallo, Billy.

**Arthur**  What are you on, then? He's saying his prayers.

**Billy**  (*scratching the ground with the cane with an assumed casualness*) No, I was just standing. Just thinking to myself. (*To Liz*) Arthur told me you were back.

**Arthur**  You looked like one of them stinking gnomes we've got in our garden. With a maring fishing rod.

*Billy tosses the garden cane into the garden*

What are you standing out here for? Won't they let you in?

**Billy**  (*irritated*) Can't I stand in my own rotten garden now? (*To Liz*) When did you get back?

**Liz**  Last week.

**Arthur**  (*before she can continue*) Hey, is it right your grandma's snuffed it?

**Billy**  You what? Yes. This afternoon. Funeral's on Tuesday.

**Arthur**  Fizzing hell! I was only talking to her this morning.

**Billy**  (*to Liz*) Why didn't you ring up?

**Arthur**  (*before she can reply*) You don't half drop me in it! I thought you'd made it up. I told our old lady you'd made it up! She'll go stinking bald.

**Billy**  (*to Liz*) You've got the number. You could have rung me up.

**Liz**  I was going to, Billy.

**Arthur**  (*again before she can continue*) Do you know what I was going to do? If I'd had enough money. I was going to send a wreath round. With a little card saying in capital letters: "You Stinking Louse-bound Crowing Liar". I was sure you'd made it up.

**Billy**  (*annoyed*) What are you talking about? What would I want to make up a thing like that for?

**Arthur**  Oh, get George Washington. (*In a mimicking falsetto*) Please sir, I cannot tell a lie. I chopped up Grandma.

**Billy**  (*turning to Arthur*) Look, why don't you just jack it in — eh?

**Arthur**  All right, all right. Keep your shirt on. Don't go biting my head off.

**Billy**  Well, you want to grow up.

**Arthur** You what! Listen who's talking. You're a right one to talk. Grow up? Blimey! (*He turns to Liz*) Do you know what he once did? He saves up these plastic boats you get out of cornflake packets. He does! He saves them all. He keeps them in his desk. Well, do you know what he once did? He filled up a baby's coffin with water — down in the basement — and started playing at naval battles. He thinks I don't know.

**Billy** Aw, shut up. Anyway, I don't sit in the lavatory all morning. Reading mucky books.

**Arthur** No, and I don't go around playing at Winston Churchills when I think nobody's looking.

**Billy** Aw, belt up, man!

**Arthur** (*tapping Billy on the chest*) You just want to stop telling people to belt up. You want to go careful, man. Or else somebody's going to belt you.

**Billy** Yeh — you and whose army?

**Arthur** I'm not talking about me. I'm talking about somebody else.

**Billy** Who?

**Arthur** Somebody's brother.

**Billy** Whose naffing brother? What are you talking about?

**Arthur** Rita's naffing brother. Who do you think? That's what I came up to tell you — thanks very much for asking. It's the last favour I'll do you, I know that. I've just seen him down at the dance hall. Screaming blue murder. I wouldn't like to be in your shoes, man, when he gets you.

**Billy** (*uneasily*) I'm not frightened of him.

**Arthur** You what! He'll bloody slaughter you. He will, you know, he's not kidding.

**Billy** So what.

**Arthur** So what, he says. I knew you should never have given her that ring in the first place. I told you, didn't I? Well, she still wants it back, you know. You've had your chips.

**Billy** Aaahh — who cares.

**Arthur** You'll bloody care when you're in the infirmary getting stitched up. Well, you've had it coming, matey, let's face it. You and your rotten lying. Well, I know what I'd do if I was you — and I didn't want to get crippled. I'd get off to that job in London, dead smartish — that's if there is a job in London.

**Billy** What do you mean — if there is a job in London?

**Arthur** I mean, if it isn't another of your stinking lies!

**Billy** I'll go — don't you worry.

**Arthur** I'm not worrying, Tosh. I've got more to do with my time. But I'll tell you this much, you can stop going round giving out the patter about our old lady. Because if I hear — once more — about her being in the family way, I'll be round here myself. Never mind Rita's brother.

**Billy** Aw — dry up.

**Arthur** (*going off*) Well, I've told you, man. (*He turns to Billy*) And don't
   think I'm covering up for you any more — 'cause I'm not.
**Billy** (*softly*) Aw — get knotted.

*Arthur goes*

   (*Turning to Liz*) He talks too much.

*There is a slight pause as they stand and look at each other*

   Hallo, Liz.
**Liz** Hallo, Billy.
**Billy** When did you get back?
**Liz** Last week.
**Billy** Why didn't you ring me up?
**Liz** I was going to.
**Billy** Thank you very much.
**Liz** No — really. I was going to. I thought I'd see you at the dance tonight.
   I went to the dance. I thought you'd be there.
**Billy** I couldn't go.
**Liz** No. No — I know. I heard about your grandma. I'm sorry.
**Billy** Yes. (*Changing the subject*) I haven't seen you for months.
**Liz** Five weeks. You didn't waste much time, did you?
**Billy** Why? What do you mean?
**Liz** Getting engaged. To everybody.
**Billy** Oh — that.
**Liz** You're mad.
**Billy** (*shrugging his shoulders*) Where have you been?
**Liz** Oh — here and there.
**Billy** Why didn't you write?
**Liz** I did — once. I tore it up.
**Billy** You're always tearing it up.
**Liz** (*changing the subject*) How's everything with you? How's the script-
   writing? How's the book coming along?
**Billy** (*enthusiastically*) Oh, I've finished it. It's going to be published next
   Christmas.

*She gives him a long, steady look*

   I haven't started writing it yet.
**Liz** You are mad.
**Billy** Yes.

*Liz sits on the garden seat*

   Liz?

**Liz** Mmmm?

**Billy** (*sitting beside her*) Do you find life complicated?

**Liz** Mmmm. So-so.

**Billy** I wish it was something you could tear up and start again. Life, I mean. You know — like starting a new page in an exercise book.

**Liz** Well, it's been done. Turning over a new leaf.

**Billy** I turn over a new leaf every day — but the blots show through.

**Liz** What's all this about London?

**Billy** I've been offered a job down there.

**Liz** Honestly?

**Billy** Honestly. A sort of job.

**Liz** Good. I'm glad. Perhaps it's your new leaf

**Billy** (*proud of the phrase*) I turn over a new leaf every day — but the blots show through the page.

**Liz** Well, perhaps a new leaf isn't good enough. Perhaps you need to turn over a new volume.

**Billy** Yes.

**Liz** Are you going to take that job?

**Billy** I think so.

**Liz** You only think so.

**Billy** I don't know.

**Liz** You know, my lad, the trouble with you is that you're — what's the word? — introspective. You're like a child at the edge of a paddling pool. You want very much to go in, but you think so much about whether the water's cold, and whether you'll drown, and what your mother will say if you get your feet wet …

**Billy** (*interrupting*) All I'm doing is wondering whether to dive or swim.

**Liz** Perhaps you need a coach.

**Billy** Do you know why I'm so fascinated by London?

**Liz** No. Why?

**Billy** A man can lose himself in London. London is a big place. It has big streets — and big people.

**Liz** (*giving him another look*) Mad.

**Billy** Perhaps I need to turn over a new paddling pool.

*There is a pause as they look at each other*

**Liz** Who do you love?

**Billy** (*adopting his thick north country accent*) Thee, lass.

**Liz** Yes, it sounds like it, doesn't it?

**Billy** I do, lass.

**Liz** Say it properly, then.

**Billy** I do, Liz, I do.

**Liz**  What about Barbara?
**Billy**  Well, what about her?
**Liz**  Well, *what* about her?
**Billy**  All over.
**Liz**  You've said that before.
**Billy**  I know. This time it is all over.
**Liz**  And what about the other one? Rita-whatever-her-name-is?
**Billy**  That's all over, too.

*There is a pause. Billy takes out a packet of cigarettes, lights two and gives one to Liz*

**Liz**  I want to marry you, you know, Billy.
**Billy**  I know, Liz — I know. We will — one day.
**Liz**  Not one day. Now.
**Billy**  Do you?
**Liz**  Next week will do. Before you go to London. Or when you get there. Whichever you prefer.
**Billy**  I think I get engaged a bit too often.
**Liz**  I don't want to get engaged. I want to get married.
**Billy**  Is that why you keep sloping off every few weeks? Because you want to get married?
**Liz**  I want to get married.
**Billy**  All right. All right.
**Liz**  How do you mean — all right? I've just proposed to you and you say "all right". Aren't you supposed to say "this is so sudden" or yes or something?
**Billy**  I don't know.

*She puts her arms round him and kisses him. He responds. They break away*

**Liz**  Billy?
**Billy**  Yes?
**Liz**  You know what you wanted me to do? That night? When we walked through the park? And I said "another night"?
**Billy**  I remember.
**Liz**  Well, it's another night tonight, isn't it?
**Billy**  (*afraid but excited*) Are you sure?
**Liz**  Yes.
**Billy**  Where could we go?
**Liz**  I've got a room. There's no-one there.
**Billy**  What do you think we ought to do about — you know, babies.
**Liz**  Have them. Lots and lots of them.
**Billy**  No, I mean tonight.

**Liz** It's all right. (*After a pause*) Billy?

**Billy** Yes?

**Liz** Ask you something?

**Billy** What?

**Liz** Do you know what *virgo intacta* means?

**Billy** Yes.

**Liz** Well, I'm not.

**Billy** No. I somehow didn't think you were.

**Liz** Want me to tell you about it?

**Billy** No. (*He kisses her*) All right, yes. Tell me about it.

**Liz** No — not now.

**Billy** Tell me about it.

**Liz** You think that's why I'm always going away, don't you?

**Billy** I don't know.

**Liz** Ask me where I've been for the past five weeks.

**Billy** What difference does it make?

**Liz** None — I suppose. It's just that every so often I want to go away. It's not you, Billy. I want to be here with you. It's the town. It's the people we know. I don't like knowing everybody — or becoming a part of things. Do you see what I mean?

**Billy** Yes ... yes.

**Liz** What I'd like is to be invisible. You know, to be able to move around without people knowing, and not having to worry about them. Not having to explain all the time.

**Billy** Liz ... Liz! Listen! Listen! Liz, do you know what I do? When I want to feel invisible. I've never told anybody. I have a sort of — well, it's an imaginary country. Where I go. It has its own people ...

**Liz** (*interrupting*) Do you do that? I knew you would. Why are we so alike, Billy? I can read your thoughts. A town like this. Only somewhere over by the sea. And we used to spend the whole day on the beach. That's what I used to think about.

**Billy** This is more than a town — it's a whole country. (*He is getting excited*) I'm supposed to be the Prime Minister. You're supposed to be the Foreign Secretary — or something.

**Liz** (*with mock obedience*) Yes, sir.

**Billy** I think about it for hours. Sometimes I think, if we were married, with a house of our own, we could just sit and imagine ourselves there.

**Liz** Yes, we could.

**Billy** I want a room, in the house, with a green baize door. It will be a big room, and when we go into it, through the door, that's it, that's our country. No-one else would be allowed in. No-one else will have keys. They won't know where the room is. Only we'll know. And we'll make models of the principal cities. You know, out of cardboard. And we could use toy soldiers. Painted. For the people. We could draw maps. It would be a place to go on a rainy afternoon. We could go there. No-one would find us. I thought we could have a big sloping shelf running all the way down one wall, you know, like a big desk. And we'd have a lot of blank paper on it and design our own newspapers. We could even make uniforms, if we wanted to. It would be our country ... (*He falters away*)

**Liz** Let's have a model train that the kids won't be allowed to use.

**Billy** Liz ... ? Will you marry me?

**Liz** Yes.

*He kisses her*

Billy?

**Billy** Yes?

**Liz** Are you really going to London or just pretending?

**Billy** I'm thinking about it.

**Liz** Only thinking?

**Billy** Well, going. Soon, anyway.

**Liz** When's soon?

**Billy** Well, soon.

**Liz** That's a bit vague. Soon. Why not now?

**Billy** It's difficult.

**Liz** No, it's easy. You just get on a train and four hours later there you are — in London.

**Billy** It's easy for you, you've had the practice.

**Liz** I'll come with you.

**Billy** That'd be marvellous — if we could.

**Liz** (*rising*) But we can, Billy! We can! What is there to stop us?

**Billy** (*thinking seriously about it for the first time*) Well, there's ... I don't know ... you've got to make all sorts of arrangements, haven't you?

**Liz** You buy a ticket, that's all. You buy a ticket and get on a train. That's all there is to it.

**Billy** I've never thought about it like that.

**Liz** Billy, we can! We can go! We can go tonight!

**Billy** But, Liz.

**Liz** There's the midnight train. We can catch that. It gets in at King's Cross Station. Breakfast at Lyons Corner House. Then we get a tube — we get a tube from Piccadilly Circus to Earl's Court. I've got friends there, Billy. They'll put us up. They'd give us a room.

**Billy** (*almost convinced; rising*) Tonight, Liz?

**Liz** Yes, tonight! Twelve-five from New Street Station. We'll be in London tomorrow. We can go to Hyde Park in the afternoon. We'll go to the pictures tomorrow night — the Odeon, Marble Arch. What time is it now?

**Billy** (*glancing at his watch*) Just after ten.
**Liz** I'm going, Billy. Are you coming?
**Billy** (*his mind made up*) Yes, Liz. I'm coming.
**Liz** Are you sure?
**Billy** I'm coming with you.
**Liz** (*briskly*) Right, then. I'm going home. Now. And I'm going to pack my things. I'll meet you at the station. In that refreshment room. In an hour's time. Eleven o'clock. I'll get the tickets. Two singles to London. You won't let me down, Billy?
**Billy** I'm coming.
**Liz** What will you tell your father and mother?
**Billy** They know already — more or less.
**Liz** You won't let them talk you out of it?
**Billy** I'm coming.

*The Lights begin to come up in the living-room*

*Geoffrey enters from the kitchen, takes up a newspaper, sits down and begins to read*

*The Lights fade slightly in the garden. Liz kisses Billy*

**Liz** Eleven o'clock.
**Billy** Eleven.

*Liz goes off down the garden*

*Billy watches her go and then turns and enters the house. Geoffrey rises at the sound of the door. Billy enters the living-room. He registers shock as he sees that his cupboard has been opened*

**Geoffrey** What time of bloody night do you call this?
**Billy** It's only ten.
**Geoffrey** I don't care what bloody time it is. Who said you could go out? And where've you been?
**Billy** I've only been out. Why? Did you want some chips bringing in?
**Geoffrey** I'll chip you. I'll chip you round your bloody ear-hole if I start on you. Have you been out dancing?
**Billy** No, 'course I haven't.
**Geoffrey** If you've been out dancing with your grandma lying dead I'll bloody murder you, I will.
**Billy** (*feigning innocence*) What's up?
**Geoffrey** What's up — you know what's up. What have you done with that letter of your mother's?

*Billy glances in fear at the envelopes on the floor*

Do you hear me? I'm talking to you!

**Billy** What letter?

**Geoffrey** What, what, what! Don't keep saying bloody "what". You know what letter. That what she gave you to post to "Housewives' Choice".

**Billy** I told her once. I posted it.

**Geoffrey** (*taking the letter from his pocket*) You posted bloody nothing. You've had it in that cupboard. It was given to you to post. You bloody idle little swine.

**Billy** I did post it. That's just the rough copy.

**Geoffrey** What are you talking about? Rough copy? It's your mother's letter. How could you have posted it?

**Billy** Look — the letter my mother wrote was full of mistakes, that's all. I just thought it would stand a better chance if I wrote it out again — properly. That's all.

*Alice enters from the kitchen*

**Geoffrey** Well, who told you to write it out again? And who told you to open it? You keep your thieving hands off other people's things! And where did you get all them bloody calendars from, as well?

**Billy** What calendars?

**Geoffrey** (*fingering his belt*) By bloody hell! I'll give you "what" if you don't stop saying "what, what," my lad! You know what! Don't think I haven't been talking to Mr Duxbury — because I have. I've heard it all. You make me a laughing-stock. You can't keep your hands off nothing. And where's that monkey wrench out of my garage? I suppose you know nothing about that?

**Billy** No, 'course I don't. What do I want with a monkey wrench?

**Geoffrey** What do you want with two hundred bloody calendars! And what have you been doing with their name-plates as well? You're not right in the bloody head.

**Billy** (*losing his temper*) I'm not right! I'm not right! I didn't want to work for Shadrack and flaming Duxbury's! You made me take the rotten job! Now you can answer for it.

**Geoffrey** Don't bloody shout at me, you gormless young get — or I'll knock your eyes out.

**Billy** God give me strength.

**Geoffrey** Give you strength, he wants to give you some sense! You're like a bloody Mary-Ann! Well, I hope your mother gets more sense out of you.

**Alice** Well, you've got yourself into a fine mess, lad, haven't you?

**Billy** Have I?

**Alice** I'm only thankful she knows nothing about it. (*She glances up at the ceiling*) Why didn't you post that letter of mine?

**Billy** I did post it. I was telling Dad. I just wrote it out again, that's all. There was some mistakes in it.

**Alice** Yes, well we can't all be Shakespeares, can we? And what's all this about you taking money from work?

**Billy** What money?

**Geoffrey** (*warningly*) I've told you.

**Billy** What? I haven't taken any money.

**Geoffrey** There's two pound ten short in your postage book. Never mind petty cash.

**Billy** Oh, that ... I ...

**Alice** What did you do with it, Billy?

**Geoffrey** He's spent it. That's what he's bloody done with it.

**Alice** Well, it's just beyond me. You didn't have to take money, Billy. You could have come to me.

**Geoffrey** You've had things too bloody easy. That's been your trouble. You can't carry on at work like you do at home, you know.

**Billy** Well, I told you I didn't want to work there when I first started, didn't I?

**Geoffrey** You didn't want to work for nobody, if you ask me anything. You thought you'd live on me, didn't you?

**Billy** No, I didn't. I could have kept myself.

**Alice** Kept yourself — how?

**Billy** Writing scripts.

**Geoffrey** Writing bloody scripts, you want to get a day's work done, never mind writing scripts. Who do you think's going to run this bloody business when I'm gone?

**Billy** You said you didn't want me in the business.

**Geoffrey** Only because you were so bloody idle! Somebody's got to carry on with it! Who's going to keep your mother?

**Billy** (*with an attempt at humour*) Why, you're not retiring, are you?

**Geoffrey** Don't try and be funny with me, lad! Or you'll laugh on the other side of your face!

**Alice** And what did you tell me about Arthur's mother? She wasn't having a baby, you know very well she wasn't.

**Billy** It was only a joke.

**Geoffrey** A joke — it sounds like a bloody joke!

**Alice** And why did you tell her I'd broken my leg?

**Billy** I didn't know you knew Arthur's mother.

**Alice** Yes, you don't know who I know and who I don't know, do you? If you want to know, she rang me up. And what did you do with that cardigan she gave you for me, last Christmas?

**Billy** (*vaguely*) I think I gave it to the refugees.

**Alice**  Well, you've got a new cardigan to find by tomorrow morning. Because she's coming round to see me.

**Billy** (*emphatically*) I won't be here tomorrow morning.

**Geoffrey**  You won't be here to bloody night if you talk to your mother in that tone of voice!

**Billy**  I'm not going to be here tonight. I'm leaving.

**Alice**  What are you talking about?

**Billy** (*decisively*) I'm getting the midnight train. Tonight. I'm taking that job in London.

**Alice**  If you're in any more trouble, Billy, it's not something you can leave behind you. You put it in your suitcase and take it with you.

**Geoffrey**  Well, he's not taking that suitcase of mine upstairs. (*Turning to Billy*) Anyway, you're not going to London or nowhere else — so you can get that idea out of your head, for a kick-off.

**Billy**  I mean it, Dad. I'm going.

**Geoffrey**  And I bloody mean it, as well. (*Raising his voice*) You stop here till that money's paid back. You can thank your lucky stars Mr Duxbury's not landed you in court. You want to be grateful.

**Billy**  Grateful! Grateful! Grateful for this, grateful for that! That's all I've ever heard! Grateful you let me go to the grammar school! We've been hearing that one since the first day I went there. What am I supposed to do? Say "thank you very much" three times a day for my marvellous education?

**Geoffrey**  Well, it's a chance we never had!

**Billy**  Yes, and don't we bloody well know it! I even had to be grateful for winning my own scholarship! And what did you say when I came running home to tell you I'd won it? Don't think I've forgotten! I was eleven years old! I came belting out of those school gates and I ran all the way! Just to tell you! And what did you say? That you'd have to pay for the uniform and I'd have to be grateful! And now I'm supposed to be grateful to Shadrack and stinking Duxbury! Why? What for? For letting me sit at one of their rotten desks all day?

**Alice** (*gently reasoning*) Well, you took the job, Billy.

**Geoffrey**  Yes, and he's stopping there till that money's paid back.

**Billy**  I'm not arguing about it. I'm going! (*He crosses towards the door*)

**Geoffrey**  Go, then! I've finished with you!

*Billy enters the hall and moves up the stairs. During the following he goes into the bedroom*

(*Crossing to the door, calling after Billy*) They'll take you to court, you know! I won't stop them! I'm not paying it back! And don't think you're taking my suitcase!

*Geoffrey crosses back into the living-room and stands silent. Alice sits in the chair by the fire*

**Alice**  Oh, dear me ... Oh, dear me.

*Billy enters from the bedroom and charges down the stairs and into the living-room*

*He is carrying a small battered suitcase. He crosses to the sideboard and, opening a drawer, begins to pack the case with shirts, socks, ties and a pullover. Geoffrey watches him in silence*

(*Concerned*) What time train do you reckon you're catching?
**Billy**  Midnight.
**Alice**  Well, what time does it get in?
**Billy**  Tomorrow morning.
**Alice**  And where are you going to live when you get there?
**Geoffrey**  He'll finish up in the Salvation Army Hostel.
**Alice**  (*as Billy packs a pair of socks*) All them socks need darning, you know.

*Billy makes no reply*

Well, you'll want more than one suit ... And what about your grandma's funeral on Tuesday?

*Billy has now placed all his clothing in the case. He stoops and begins to pack the calendars*

**Geoffrey**  (*in disbelief*) What the thump are you packing them bloody calendars for?
**Billy**  I thought I'd post them.
**Alice**  Well, you'll be expected at the funeral, you know.
**Geoffrey**  (*disparagingly*) He's not going anywhere.
**Billy**  (*slamming the case shut, rising*) I'm going.

*He picks up the case and crosses to the door*

**Geoffrey**  (*half relenting*) Don't act so bloody daft.

*Billy pauses for a moment, his hand on the door, caught up in the embarrassment of leaving*

**Billy**  Well, I'll write to you then. Soon as I've got fixed up. (*Acutely embarrassed*) I'm sorry about my grandma.

*He goes out*

**Alice** Oh, dear me ... Oh, dear me.

**Geoffrey** They can summons him. I've finished.

**Alice** You'll have to pay it, Geoffrey. Will he be all right on his own?

**Geoffrey** He won't bloody go — he'll be back in five minutes.

**Alice** We know nothing about where he's going and what he's supposed to be doing. Who's that fellow he says he's going to work for? That comedian?

**Geoffrey** I don't bloody know.

**Alice** It was in that letter he had in his pocket in that old raincoat.

*Geoffrey crosses and takes the envelope from the raincoat which is hanging in the hall. He returns into the living-room reading the letter to himself as he walks. He then reads the letter aloud to Alice*

**Geoffrey** "Dear Mr Fisher, Many thinks for script and gags, I can use some of the gags and pay accordingly. As for my staff job, well I regret to tell you, I do not have staff beside my agent, but several of the boys do work for me, you might be interested in this. (*He pauses*) Why not call in for a chat next time you are in London? Best of luck and keep writing. Danny Boon."

**Alice** (*after pause*) Run down to the station and fetch him back.

**Geoffrey** He's off his bloody rocker.

**Alice** You'll have to go stop him, Geoffrey.

**Geoffrey** Nay, he's big enough to look after himself now. He can stand on his own two feet for a change. I've finished. I've done my whack for him.

**Alice** I wonder if he's got any money?

**Geoffrey** That's his look-out. It doesn't belong to him if he has. You can depend on that.

**Alice** Oh, dear me ... Oh, dear me.

**Geoffrey** There's no need for him to starve. He can get a job if he sets his mind to it. And gets up in a morning.

**Alice** Well, what's he going to do?

**Geoffrey** He can go clerking — same as here. There's a lot of offices in London. Well, there's one thing certain. I know what I'm going to bloody do: I'm off to bed. I've enough on my plate without worrying my head over that one. He can go to hell, he can.

**Alice** Do you want a cup of Ovaltine, or anything?

**Geoffrey** No. You want to get off to bed as well, lass.

**Alice** (*rising*) I always used to take her one up at this time. I'll have to get used to it — not having to.

**Geoffrey** Aye, well ...

**Alice** Is the back door locked, Geoffrey?

**Geoffrey** I've seen to it.

*They cross into the hall. Geoffrey switches off the light in the living-room and automatically drops the catch on the Yale lock. Geoffrey follows Alice up the stairs. As they go up the porch light fades up*

*Rita and Arthur enter the garden*

(*With assumed cheerfulness*) Well, he'll come home at holiday times. And happen some weekends.

*Geoffrey switches out the hall light from the top of the stairs and follows Alice into the bedroom*

**Arthur** (*with relief, seeing the hall light go out*) They've gone to bed.
**Rita** Have a look through the rotten letter-box.
**Arthur** You can see! They've gone to bed. You don't think they're sitting there with no lights on, do you?
**Rita** Well, he's not getting out of it — 'cause I shall come round in the morning. Our kid'll come round as well. Our kid'll duff him up. He'll get that ring back.
**Arthur** You and your kid and that louse-bound ring! Come on, let's get down to Foley Bottoms. Get some snogging hours in.
**Rita** He needn't think he's got away with it — 'cause he hasn't. He'll be a stretcher case tomorrow morning. (*She screams up at the bedrooms*) You'll be a stretcher case tomorrow morning! You wait! You rotten yellow-bellied squint-eyed get! You're nothing else! You closet!

*We hear the sound of a window being flung open and Alice shouting*

**Alice** Get away! Don't you know we've got somebody dead in this house!

*We hear the window slammed shut*

**Rita** (*screaming*) You want to be all rotten dead You want gassing!
**Arthur** Shut up, Rita! She knows my mother.
**Rita** I don't care.
**Arthur** They're not worth bothering about. Come on — let's get down to Foley Bottoms. We're just wasting time stuck here.
**Rita** (*allowing Arthur to place his arm around her and pilot her out of the garden*) Well, we'll be round here first thing tomorrow morning. (*As they go*) We get up before they do.

*Arthur and Rita go off*

*There is a pause and then Billy enters and walks slowly and dejectedly to the front door. He puts down his case and, taking a key from his pocket, opens the door and enters. He crosses into the living-room and, closing the door behind him, switches on the light. He stands indecisively for a moment and then crosses and switches on the radio. He crosses to his suitcase and opens it as the sound of a dance-band comes from the radio. He stands for a moment and, as the music continues, he compulsively lifts his hand and begins to conduct. He glances towards the ceiling, wondering if he is making too much noise, then crosses and switches off the radio. He returns to the suitcase which he carries over to the sideboard. He opens his cupboard and is neatly stacking the calendars back into the cupboard*

CURTAIN

# PROPERTY PLOT

## ON STAGE

*On sofa*
  **Granny**'s handbag
  In it:
    Sweets
    Ration book
    Pension book
    Hospital card
    Spectacles
    Small purse
    Three letters
*On table*
  Runner
  Ashtray
  Chenille cloth
*On sideboard*
  Radio
  Ashtray
  Two vases
  Invoices in vase
  Pencil
  Notepad
  Spare key under radio
*In sideboard*
  Clothes in drawers
  Sock in US drawer
  Smelling salts in DS drawer
  Calendars in US cupboard
  Blue letter in US cupboard

Crepe bandage in US cupboard
Books in DS cupboard
Spectacles in DS cupboard
*In cocktail cabinet*
  Port
  Glasses
*At fireplace*
  Companion set
*On mantelpiece*
  Clock
  Pipe rack
  Six pipes
  Pouch of tobacco
  Spectacles in case
  Ashtray
  Matches
  Pipe cleaners on wall
*On armchair*
  **Geoffrey**'s jacket
*In hall*
  Telephone
  Directory
  Newspaper in letterbox
  **Alice**'s hat on hook
  **Geoffrey**'s hat on hook
  **Geoffrey**'s mac on hook
  Spare coat on hook

## OFF STAGE

*In kitchen*
  Cup and saucer
  Plate
  Teaspoon
  Knife
  Second cup, saucer and spoon
  Jar of jam
  Bread in paper
  Butter in paper
  Pot of tea — on curtain up
  Jug of milk
  Basin of sugar
  Sugar spoon

Pint milk bottle — half full
Magnesia in tumbler
Spoon in tumbler
Notepad
Pencil
Egg in eggcup
Blue letter
One duster on sweeper handle
Two tea towels on rack
One hand towel on rack
Carpet sweeper
Pedal bin
Shopping bag

**Alice**'s handbag
**Alice**'s gloves
**Alice**'s coat on hook
*Off* c (*Upstairs*)
  **Billy**'s:
    Suit
    Shirt
    Pants
    Socks
    Shoes
    Tie
    Comb
    Watch
    Suitcase

*Off left*
  **Barbara**'s handbag
    In it:
      Six oranges
      Four large tissues
      One comb
      Small box of Kleenex
      Bottle of pills
*In garden*
  Seat
  Four canes (one in plant)
*Check*
  Curtains open
  Cocktail cabinet unclipped
  Yale lock on catch

## FIRST INTERVAL

*Strike*
  Two glasses from cabinet
  Orange from floor
  Orange from cabinet
  Re-cork port
  Close cocktail cabinet
  Orange peel from white bag
  Tissues from white bag
  Runner from table
  Raincoat from behind sofa to
    hooks in hall
  Pyjamas from behind sofa
  Crepe bandage from floor
  Blue letter from sideboard
*From kitchen*
  Two dirty cups and saucers
  Dirty plate and knife
*Check*
  Ration book in bag
  Pipes on mantelpiece
  All doors closed
  Armchair on marks

*Set*
  Furniture to red marks
*On table*
  Tea cloth
  Four cups and saucers
  Five small plates
  Five small glass dishes on plates
  Nine teaspoons
  One glass dish — six pieces of tinned
    orange in it
  Three pieces of tinned orange in small
    dish
  One teapot
  One milk jug
  One pint pot
  Five paper napkins (crumpled)
  Tray in kitchen
*By armchair*
  **Granny**'s handbag
*On sofa*
  White handbag with clean tissues

## SECOND INTERVAL

*Strike*
White handbag from DS of sofa
**Granny**'s handbag from sideboard

Two bundles of calendars from sideboard

*Check*
  Cane

Pipe
All doors closed
Raincoat in hall
Letter in raincoat
*Set*
  Sideboard open
  Re-bundle calendars into four
    bundles and twelve loose
  Set clock at 9.30
  Set armchair to new mark
  Garden seat to marks
  Close curtains
*On draining board*
  Tray, on it:
    Two cups and saucers
    Two spoons
    Jug of milk
    Basin of sugar
    Sugar spoon
    Plate of biscuits
  Kettle of hot water US of sink
  Gate off latch

*In sideboard*
  Two large bundles of calendars
  In US cupboard
  Toy boat in DS cupboard
*On floor near cupboard*
  Two large bundles of calendars
  Twelve loose calendars
  Fez
  Toy policeman
  Two toy guns
  Hair brush
  Apricot box
  Plane
  Snow scene
  Three books
  Coloured cap
  Field glasses
  Two magazines
  Comic
  Two coconuts
  Other toys,
  etc.

MADE AND PRINTED IN GREAT BRITAIN BY
LATIMER TREND & COMPANY LTD PLYMOUTH
MADE IN ENGLAND